The
Enneagram

The Sacred Enneagram In The

Christian Perspective

By Morgan Rohr

<u>**Table of Contents**</u>

Introduction

Congratulations for purchasing *The Enneagram: The Sacred Enneagram in the Christian Perspective* and thank you for doing so.

The following chapters will discuss a history of the Enneagram symbol, its relevance to Christianity, a description of each of the types, and an eclectic methodology to help you unlock the meaning of each of the personality types in order to increase self-awareness and improve your interpersonal and inner life.

There are plenty of books on this subject on the market, thanks again for choosing this one! Every effort was made to ensure it is full of as much useful information as possible, please enjoy!

Chapter : 1
The Sacred Enneagram: Historical Origins

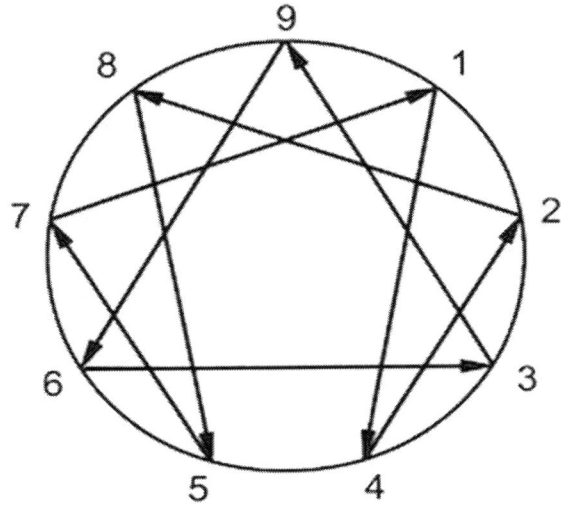

The history of the Enneagram of Personality is widely disputed, but there are some main points that are agreed upon as major contributing factors. There certainly seem to be roots that can seem be traced back at to the philosophy of Ancient Greece. Some will emphasize the mathematical and geometrical qualities and evoke Pythagoras and Boethius; others point to its connections to the tradition of Kabbalah. These various traditions make up the framework that expresses the intrinsic archetypes that can be found in the Enneagram of Personality, and serve as perspectives and traditions to consider when approaching the use of the Enneagram for self-development. The Enneagram's ancient history provides the basis for its relevance with Christianity; many of these sources had been influences on Christian thinking from the very beginning.

Platonic Essentialism serves as a founding for many of the archetypes and symbolic systematology involved in the foundations of the Enneagram. Basically, this comes from the philosophy of Aristotle and Plato and, it states that every person has an "essence." This "essentialism" is a core human concept that alludes to the Essence of the soul, and it was germinated in Greece and Asia Minor. Eventually the ideas moved, as spices and materials did, geologically south, to areas now known as Syria and even further to Egypt. It was in these places that the ideas were adopted by early Christian mystics who focused on the ways that the divine form was lost in the ego. This is the origin of the Christian concept of the seven deadly sins. The original inspiration for the Christian seven deadly sins was contained by the same material that contained the nine types in the Enneagram.

Most scholars agree that it was the Sufis, people from sect of Islam that emphasizes mysticism and ecstasy, who developed the concept of personality types. They were a spiritual and mystical people, who did a lot of work in the area of spiritual research. The Sufis' culture was deeply ingrained with mysticism. It was under their influence in the 14th and 15th centuries that the idea of personalities become defined. It was a Sufi belief that there were nine essential patterns or orientations to life. These patterns and orientations represented the image of God that exists within that person. There is also the other side of this representation: the opposite force within the person, which serves to block the realization of the power within.

The Sufis had a tradition of spiritual development that encouraged people to find their way to God over many years, and they witnessed from direct observation the nine ways in which peoples' personalities manifest, and how they run in to obstacles in their journey. To condense the Sufi's primary question, one could put it like this: What happens? What happens to our original goodness? What happens along the way to cause us to be distracted, or anxious, or too angry to have clarity in our lives?

The Sufis' believed that our psychological and spiritual development – our experiences, our upbringing, our attitudes and positioning in the world – grow a tension between two dualistic truths that are available to each aspect of us: the virtue, or essential truth that mimics the divine form, or the vice, which serves to distort and subvert each virtue.

Think about the way that our upbringing and context influences the way our personality is expressed. If a child grows up in a chaotic household, an environment in which she must protect herself, then she will develop ways to protect herself. The most developed and often used parts of the child's personality will be the ones that serve as protection. This could manifest itself in many ways, whether the strategies are good for the child or not.

Once these behaviors and attitudes are firmly established, a person feels like they have an identity, and the ego starts to take hold. We then develop strategies to protect the undeveloped parts from criticism.

The Sufis had a beautiful long tradition of meditation and prayer and mysticism. This path toward spiritual guidance led the Sufis to integrate many concepts with spirituality. As their mathematical capabilities grew in the fifteenth century, Sufi mathematicians discovered the decimal system. This led to the concept of periodic decimal fractions (when one is divided by three or seven). As their scientific and mathematical understanding of the world grew, this knowledge was incorporated and fused into their spiritual understanding, and the Enneagram was one of the products of this marriage of science and faith. In the nine points of energy that the

Enneagram describes, the Sufis saw nine refractions of the one divine love. The word enneagram itself comes from the Greek words ennea (nine) and gramma (letter).

The Sufis' understood the potential for insight in exploring our vices. The Sufi tradition asks "What do our negative qualities teach us?" and it encourages the idea that positive and enriching value can be gleaned from exploring our negative sides. Before we can move on and understand ourselves, we have to look at how we are benefitting from the vices.

Kabbalah is a mystical ancient strain of Judaism. It is at once a school of thought, a method, and a discipline of Judaism. It contains the Tree of Life. The Tree of Life is a symbol in Kabbalah that is said to be a map illustrating various aspects of the world and our experience in it. The Tree of Life offers another interpretation of the divine forms which are manifested in our behaviors. The Kabbalah has nine Sefirot, which correlate with the Enneagram. Point One aligns with Hochma (all knowing, correct, internalized father, Abba), Point Two with Bina (understanding, controlling, supernal mother, ima,) Point Tree with Gedula (impetus to be great) Point Four with Tiferet (beauty, romantic longing, point five with Din (bound, enclosed, limited) Point Six with nezeh (enduring seeking authority), point seven with Hod (splendor), Point Eight with Yeysod (seminal force) and point nine with shechina (accepting presence).

Because of its wide-reaching, possibly universal roots, the enneagram seems to be mostly congruent with most major religious traditions. The enneagram is known in the Christian tradition to be a bridge between spirituality and psychology. With some research, we can see how the system of the Enneagram fits in with multiple secular and sacred sources regarding vices and virtue, or intelligences and weaknesses. Multiple ancient personality systems are contained in variants of the Enneagram model in Christianity, Sufism and Judaism implies that the Enneagram has an ancient and common resonance with may peoples of earth. In the table below, four ideological interpretations are made of concepts contained in the Enneagram.

Enneagram	Kabbalah	apital Sins	DSM-V
1.) The Perfectionist	Hochma – All knowing, correct	Anger	Compulsive
2.) The Giver	Bina-Understanding, supernal	Pride	Histrionic

	mother		
3.) The Performer	Gedula – Impetus to be great	Deceit (self)	Narcissist (secondary)
4.) The Romantic	Tiferet - beauty, romantic longing	Envy	Depressive
5.) The Investigator	Din-Bound, enclosed	Avarice	Avoidant
6.) The Loyalist	Nezeh-seeking authority	Fear	Paranoid
7.) The Enthusiast	Hod--splendor	Gluttony	Narcissist (primary)

8.) The Protector	Yesod-Seminal force	Lust	Sociopath
9.) The Peacemaker	Shecihina-accepting presence	Sloth	Obsessive-compulsive

Ivonovich Gurdjeff has a significant place in the history of the Enneagram. He was a Russian adventurer and seeker who had studied Tibetan, Sufi, Indian and Christian mysticism. Interestingly, Gurdjieff became aware of the enneagram in Afghanistan. Gurdjieff didn't use the enneagram as typology of personality, however. He saw it as a sort of philosopher's stone, which had deep resonance in the archetypal experience of humanity. Gurdjieff's enneagram seems to have come somewhat directly from the Kabbalistic Tree of Life. Gurdjieff's studies laid the foundation for Oscar Ichaz0's work.

The most modern significant phase of the development of theory around the Enneagram was in the 1960's and 70's, during the work of philosopher Oscar Ichazo. Ichazo was native to South America, and after visiting various parts of Asia, he returned to Buenos Aires to develop his ideas, and eventually created the Arica School. The Arica School consisted of a system of psychology influenced by metaphysics and spirituality, based on the centuries of enrichment around the Enneagram symbol, created to help people reach new levels of self-realization. Ichazo's new conception of the Enneagram acknowledges influence of mystical Judaism, Christianity, Islam, Buddhism, and ancient Greek Philosophy. He saw his work as a way to make clear the relationship between our essential selves and our ego-selves; to Ichazo, there is a potential in each human to be at harmony with the world, to be thriving against its challenges and settling in when there its comfort and ease.

The Enneagram is a topology; it is not unique in this, and there are various other systems of typology for personality. Astrology, for example, finds twelve categories for types. Psychologist Carl Jung, in his writings, uses the premise that there are three pairs of functions that are expressed differently in each person: extroversion-introversions, perception-intuition, and thinking-feeling. In each case, a person will favor one of each, leaving us with eight distinct personality types. Jung's archetypes also support and enrich the Enneagram. Jung's archetypes and how they relate to the types of the Enneagram will be discussed later.

The Myers'-Briggs typology is one that has been widely used since its conception. Isabel Briggs Myers developed this system by considering a different set of functions. Those are judging-perceiving, the inclination to quick, clear judgments and decisions as opposed to receptivity to many influences and kinds of information. She eventually developed the Myers-Briggs Type Indicator, a test that distinguishes among the sixteen types that are present there.

The psychoanalyst Fritz Riemann was influenced by astrology when he worked out a scheme of human fears. He assumes four basic human fears: the fear of nearness, fear of distance, fear of change, and fear of permanence. This results in Riemann's four basic types: Schizoid, depressive, compulsive, and hysterical.

The guiding principle for all of these different models of personality classification is that all people are different, but that some individuals have experiences and behaviors and attitudes that are remarkably similar. to one another. A typology can be thought of as a sort of map, that has the purpose of facilitating and overview of the soul. The Enneagram is a circle whose circumference is broken up by nine points. The points are numbered clockwise from 1 to 0. Points 3, 6, and 9 are bound together in a triangle, as are 1, 4, 2, 8, and 5, and 7 in a hexagon.

Chapter : 2
The Nine Types

The Enneagram of Personality describes nine contrasting worldviews and perspectives. These can be seen as strategies to navigate the journey of life. They can also be described as patterns. The theory of these personality types isn't that they describe a perfect individual or a bad individual; in each of the types is contained a pattern that develops in many ways and directions. For example, the Protector, or Type Seven, has the capacity to use their power and intensity for incredible good and the wellbeing of others, or for unspeakable evil. The characteristics that go with each type can be considered coping mechanisms, or habits, strategies; the can be developed in a skillful manner or an unskillful one. In the initial description of each type, there are some classifications. The Triad, which will be explored in more depth later, describes some of the basic drives and fears of the nine types divided into three groups. The Spiritual Focus of the type is where they find their general focus as an individual most of the time, for better or worse. The Strength is an example of one common adaptive characteristic of the type, and the Weakness is one example of a maladaptive characteristic of the type. The Positive Direction describes a positive path for growth that is commonly seen among the specified individuals. The Essence is about a person's positioning in the world, the authentic way they see beauty in the world. This brings us to the Secure Embodiment and the Stress Embodiment. Types tend to shift a little in personality to embody characteristics of other types when they are stressed, and similarly, people will also change their personality when they are feeling secure and positive. The Secure

Embodiment shows which personality type any given type will shift to when they are at their best. The Stress Embodiment shows how a certain type will change when they are feeling worried, anxious, stressed, or otherwise unhealthy. The last category in the initial description types is the Wings of each personality type. For each type, they tend to act more like the types situated right next to them on the circle than the other types. For example, a Seven will act more like an Eight and a Six than any of the other types. They are closer in the way they perceive the world. Take a look at the descriptions for each of the type, and consider how you and other people you know relate to them.

Type One is The Perfectionist.

- Triad: Defender
- Spiritual Focus: Correcting error, a right/wrong mindset

- Strength: Moral compass
- Weakness: Error
- Positive Direction: From criticality and judging to serenity
- Essence: Perfection
- Secure Embodiment: The Enthusiast
- Stress Embodiment: The Romantic
- Wings: The Peacemaker and The Giver

High-Profile Case Example:

Mahatma Ghandi

Ghandi was an extreme example of the Type One. He had such a deep drive to stand for morality and truth that he dedicated his life to the good. Ghandi was punished and imprisoned for his actions against the British colonial rule. He laid down his life to address what he believed in as the ultimate good.

Personality Case Example 1

Deirdre is a business manager at a large local credit union. She oversees the majority of their operations, and is responsible for a great deal of oversight. Deirdre is known as a meticulous woman, who plays it safe, and pays attention o the details. She does her best when she can fill his life with organization and timeliness, and she likes things to be neat. It took her a few years after she started working that his current environment to get her office how she likes it. She likes design that is minimalist and simple. Deirdre really dislikes distracting noises, and moved her private office to the other side of the building from the busy lobby. Her office is very peaceful; sounds are muffled, and it has a sense of privacy.

Neatness and order is a prerequisite to work with Deirdre. The top of her polished desk reflects the sun shining perfectly through the window, which has not a speck of detectable dust or smudge. The office plants are well kept and beautiful. Files are very delicately labeled, and everything is coded by color and format.

Deirdre is sometimes required to be a sort of salesperson; she despises this. Usually, she is able to push those duties off to sometime else. However, even when she does, she provides strict supervision, to make sure that every aspect of the business is running well. She writes extremely detailed memos. Everything needs to be very clear, so that the message is understandable and will not be misinterpreted. Since she started as the business manager, the credit union's operations have been running more smoothly than ever before. What she has brought to the company is a sense of accountability and responsibility.

On Saturday nights, you can find Deirdre at the Howling Moon, a local pub and music venue, playing fiddle at the bluegrass music open jam. She and other bluegrass musicians gather to pick and play songs, to share laughter, and to practice their skills. Almost nobody knows that Deirdre does this. She finds it a huge release to play her fiddle in the dim-lit hall, improvising and sometimes even singing till late at night.

Personality Case Example 2

Steven is the head supervisor at a contracting firm in Colorado. It is a rural area, and often the job includes traveling around their remote region of the state to take jobs. He is often on the road driving for hours. He doesn't mind this, however; he finds that he can still be productive on car rides. He sometimes will record instructions on his phone, or spend the time on conference calls with clients or coworkers. Steven sometimes will listen to recordings of motivational talks or self-improvement programs in his truck on these long drives. Sometimes, he'll put on a Willie Nelson album, and get lost in thought, but only sometimes.

Steven has a good sense of instinct on how to present himself. He wouldn't be able to answer how he as arrived at this, but he just knows what works and what doesn't. He can wear his Carhartt coveralls when meeting with ranchers out in the hills, but when he travels to Denver, he puts on his cowboy hat, nice shirt, and bolo tie. Steven is surprisingly judgmental sometimes of people who are not dressed appropriately for an occasion. He'll see someone and label him or her as "bum" or "silly kids". Usually he keeps his critiques to himself, but sometimes he becomes angry, and those who work with him know that his judgments can be harsh.

Once, a foreman had accused him of being callous, and Steven really felt the sting of this comment. It felt like a damaging truth that could be used against him. Sometimes Steven has difficulty keeping workers around; they tend to lack a sense of trust in him. He doesn't trust his coworkers, but the has a need to make sure that everything is exactly right, and often checks after people's work too much. He feels that his is responsible for every single detail.

Steven has noticed how much criticism affects him, and tries to be gentle when he is criticizing others. It's just part of his nature to obsess over things.

Issues aside, Steven has an excellent reputation as a supervisor and has defended the company on countless occasions when things got tough. He also defends his workers from the sometimes unrealistic demands of the higher-ranking managers at his company. He makes sure that the system he works for is fair.

The Type Ones are idealists, striving for truth, justice, fairness, honesty, and moral order. They are often very good leaders, but have trouble accepting their imperfections and the imperfections of others, offering too much criticism of themselves and others.

Family of origin and the childhood experience are always integral parts of why a person is the way they are. The Perfectionist generally tried to be a model citizen from very early on. In early childhood, The Perfectionists were told to be good, behave yourself, try hard and work hard, don't be childish, do it better. Often the parents of a Perfectionist will be moralistic, or eternally dissatisfied. They may find difficulty in praising their children to the appropriate degree, or take above-average goodness for granted. The perfectionist learned to produce this "goodness" because they were afraid of losing the love of the parent. The Perfectionist will find themselves with the fear of losing attention and love; will meet the excessive expectations of their mother and/or father.

Type Ones try to be good so that they won't be punished. As The Perfectionist moves into adulthood, they will often find that they have internalized the voices of these demanding figures in their childhood. The voices may evoke thoughts of "self-sacrificing," good, or generous. The ultimate question that these voices are often asking is "are you good enough?" Inside the Perfectionist, court is always in session. The prosecution is bringing up all of these examples of when the person was not good enough, how they could never be good enough. The defendant, strong at first, offers up some instances where the person did enough, but never quite wins the case.

Now, there's a bit of moralism, idealism, and perfectionism in almost everyone, but the type one takes this instinct front and center when dealing with the world. Thus, the Perfectionist's key vice is the search for perfection. Sometimes, a Perfectionist will have a beautiful experience, one they are completely taken in by; this could be a beautiful sunset, a perfect painting or piece of music, or a person. A Perfectionist will meet someone who appears to them to be perfect at first- in the

Perfectionists' mind; they fill the requirements of a perfect person. As the relationship progresses, the type one will eventually find the flaws of the person, and become disappointed. A common tendency for Type ones is for them to become unhappy because the world around them is not what they think it should be.

Anger is the root of the key vice in The Perfectionist. The Perfectionist is ashamed of their anger, their flaws, and the avoidance kicks in. Anger is something imperfect. This puts most Type Ones in a place of dilemma, then: they feel anger because the world is not perfect, but cannot express that anger, because showing anger makes them believe they are not perfect.

In extreme cases, The Perfectionist may be living a double life. In public, they are spotless, moral, and blameless. But in somewhere in the person's life, the repressed darkness shows itself, whether it turns out to be behavior, thinking, or disorder in other ways.

The reverse of the search for perfection is cheerful tranquility. This can be a great way for Type Ones to battle their search for perfection. Cheerful tranquility could also be described in part by the Buddhist-sourced idea or loving kindness, a part of the mindfulness tradition. When a type one strives for loving kindness or cheerful tranquility, they are letting themselves slow down, soften up, and accept what things are without wanting them to be different.

Type Two is The Giver.

- Triad: Attacher
- Spiritual Focus: Needs of Others
- Strength: True giving
- Weakness: Own needs
- Positive Direction: From pride to humility
- Essence: Freedom
- Secure Embodiment: The Romantic
- Stress Embodiment: The Protector
- Wings: The Perfectionist and the Performer

High-Profile Case Example:

Mother Theresa

Mother Theresa was a Catholic nun and missionary. She founded the Missionaries of Charity, which is a huge organization that funds and organizes missions revolving around helping others. She, like Ghandi, directed her entire life towards the recognition of the good, fighting for morality. Mother Theresa, however, worked a little differently. Rather than fighting against the law, she dedicated her service to working directly with individuals. This is the tendency of the Giver: to give themselves to others.

Personality Case Example

Charlie teaches eight year olds in the third grade. This is what he wanted to do from childhood. He can remember pretending to the be teacher when playing with friends, lining up the neighborhood children in rows while he stood and delivered the lecture from a toy blackboard, a present he had received from his parents. He found himself a caretaker even back then. He earned verbal approval from the kids' parents, who thought he was adorable, ad also from her parents and teachers. As a young boy, Charlie would stay behind after school so that he could help a teacher carry books to their car. However, he was choosy; he didn't help all of the teachers, only the ones who he judged would keep up the relationship. He never helped the art teacher.

He was a model student in college. Charlie chose to participate in activities in college that would build his resume in the most efficient way, but kept himself busy with volunteering work, secretary of the rugby club, and other extracurricular responsibilities. He was recognized and popular with his peers and teachers, and he kept his pride for being able to be a facilitator and giver secret.

Charlie always knew what type of environment he wanted to create in the classroom. Now, he had been teaching in classrooms for thirteen years. His current classroom was created to be comfortable and to feel safe for the kids. There were art supplies, plush carpet, stimulating materials, instruments, computers, all provided to the students in an organized and safe world. He loves to be the gateway to higher education for children, recognizing their strengths and encouraging them to try new things.

While he is aware of the praises and compliments that he receives behind his back, Charlie does not admit this to himself or others. Charlie knows deep down that he is a human and cannot be the most indispensable teacher in the world, but he tries to imagine that it is possible. He takes on many extra duties and helps far above anyone else in the school. He might even feel competitive sometimes, when a third party appears to be providing as much help and assistance as he does. He loves to see previous students when they come back to drop by.

Dawn is 45. She's gregarious and affable, and has been practicing as a psychologist for fifteen years. She's been a bulwark of security and helpfulness at her behavioral therapy center that she has worked at for the last ten. Originally, she studied psychology because she had heard the term "helping profession", to refer to counselors and therapists. She had known from early in life that she liked to help people. She was always the one who gave of herself. She took very good care of other friends and family.

Dawn held her job in extremely high regard; she found it worth celebrating that she was given the honor of an established position working with people to help the. She is rock steady in her reliability. Others have come and gone, but Dawn has stayed working at the behavioral health center for ten years uninterrupted. She has seen how different personalities work with the clients, and is always the g0-to when students or younger professionals have trouble with documentation or other written matters. Dawn has had the opportunity to be promoted to the director of the center more than once, but has refused. She loves the opportunity to work directly with people rather than having the responsibilities of the first-in-command.

Dawn does like, however, when people express their need for her. The amount of work that she does at the center does not go unnoticed, and many feel like they couldn't do what they do without Dawn. This is very motivational for Dawn, and she gets a sense of approval from others this way.

Her center provides a variety of services and Dawn takes on clients from all walks of life. Sometimes clients will have experienced cases of severe trauma, or have drug or alcohol problems. Sometimes, people have minor depression, or are just over-stressed. Dawn feels very present and in the individual sessions even more than the group work. She cares very deeply for other people. The clients can see this and it has helped many people to change. Dawn also volunteers at a local food bank, and seems to have a natural ability to make people smile. She has a strength that pervades a room and makes everyone feel cared for. She knows this is true but would never admit this to herself or others.

Type Twos, The Givers, often will seek out relationships and work that aligns with their need to help others and give to others. They may find themselves in the professions of education, healthcare, or psychology. They stand by others when they have to endure suffering, pain, or conflict. This gives The Giver a sense that they have a place in the world, and that someone else is with them to help them (or need them) when they need it. The Giver often has faults that may be more difficult to see than other types. They may find that they have an excessive need for validation. They may find that their childhood experience was one of emptiness or sadness. This can be an environment that was lacking in security or empathy. Oftentimes, the Giver experienced a family of origin in which the love was conditional. They needed to fulfill a role in order to have love. Sometimes when people grow up in these conditions, they find it hard to look back realistically on their situation, and may find that they have a rose-colored glasses view of their childhood. once they look closer, however, they early on had a feeling of having to be asuport for the emotional needs of other family members. They had the feeling that they had to make themselves useful in order to be noticed and loved. Unlike The Perfectionist, the Giver doe not get hung-up on being "good". They want to be nice and helpful. They sometimes are convinced that they are just that, and no more than that. A caricature of a mother of a Giver may say something like "All that I've done for you, and now you do this!".

The giver is continually holding their finger to the wind to determine its direction; they are often times too influenced by their environment. Whatever the people around them say they are, they are.

A child who is a type tow will make a grand entrance into the room, announcing their presence. They will be rewarded for this with attention and love, and respond with vibrancy. When the attention fades, however, the type two fades, and becomes despondent and loses the energy.

When The Giver enters adulthood, they need to adjust to the real needs and relationship that come with. Often times, when a Giver has not been able to adjust their orientation as an adult, they will find themselves being needy and possessive. They seem to be saying, "Let me help you" but really the message is closer to "need me". Obviously, this can lead The Giver to be manipulated; many can see that the Giver has a propensity to give and give and not want anything in return except neediness.

This problem is one of identity. The Giver will change continually in order to meet the needs of whatever person is present. This leads for the giver to have multiple selves, which leads to a problem of integration of self.

In their partnerships, Tows may be very possessive. They may end up with partners who are weak or dependent. A classic constellation is the partnership between a Giver and an addict. Codependence is usually in play here, as the Giver helps the addict, puts up with everything, forgives them, and gives multiple chances. This of course, enables the addict to keep up with their addiction. The are capable of being sweet and pliant until the moment occurs when the become very afraid of losing their place in love.

When someone finds himself or herself embodying these aspects of the Giver, they should find a way to surrender themselves. This is the pride of a Giver. They wanted to be everyone's garbage disposal, but when it is their turn to give up parts of themselves that are vulnerable, they re not able to take the place of the dependent one. This is a fear of rejections and sometimes the feeling that nobody likes me anyway. The key vice for Type tows is pride. We see Type Tows having a difficult time finding real self-knowledge and eschewing it for an easier self-analysis that they are meant to be only for others and not themselves.

The Giver has a hard time taking risks. This can serve to protect this individual from harm, but also prevents a person from achieving what they might be able to achieve. They see sharing their own thoughts and feelings as risky. A sense of rejection or disapproval is a real bitter taste for a Giver. It goes against their nature.

In order to be on a path of growth, the Giver will often need to learn to experience their emotions more intensely. They will have to give up being a helper for a little while and focus on themselves. If the Giver does this, they will find that they can direct some of their helping power inward. This is very freeing for the Giver to experience, and they might find joy in this practice. It will allow them to be better supports for others.

Type Three is The Performer.

- Triad: Attacher
- Spiritual Focus: Tasks
- Weakness: Failure
- Strength: Leadership on behalf of others
- Positive Direction: From self-deceit to honesty
- Essence: Hope
- Secure Embodiment: The Investigator
- Stress Embodiment: The Peacemaker
- Wings: The Giver and the Romantic

High-Profile Case Example:

Arnold Schwarzenegger

Arnold Schwarzenegger has been a household name for decades now, and for good reason. An Austrian immigrant, Schwarzenegger rose in the international ranks as a bodybuilder and created a career for himself that centered around performance and achievement. He went on to become one of the most known performers in American film, and even a California governor. His is the type of personality that never rests, until the highest levels of performance have been met.

Personality Case Example

John is known in the culinary world around his town as an incredible chef. At the age of twenty-four, just our of a top culinary school, he was appointed sous chef at an famous upscale sushi restaurant in Los Angeles. John spent summers during his education cutting his teeth in the restaurant industry in California. He was a charismatic leader even then, and he was easygoing and easy to relate to.

Immediately as sous chef, John proved himself to be worthy of the position, going above and beyond the duties to which he was assigned, often putting in extra hours or implementing new details that the chef had never seen before. He gathered a loyal following in the community as a talented young chef.

Soon, John was hired to be a head chef at another prominent restaurant in Los Angeles, where he worked closely with another well-known chef who had years more experience than john. John developed excellent interpersonal skills, and grew a huge network of fellow professionals and peers.

John now excels in various work environments, where he consults for successful restaurant businesses around the country and the world, and always seems to be reaching higher and higher in his achievement.

Personality Case Example 2

Morty is known as a role model in his occupation. He is an incredible scholar, leader, and even athletic. When he was in school, he achieved to the highest degree, consistently making it to every class, determined to be the best. His first job was as a math teacher in a small but well-known private middle school. In addition to a full course load, he helped teach the film class and coached the cross-country team. He was married with a couple kids at this time, and after a couple years in the classroom; he took on ever-increasing responsibility in the administrative department, until his third year when he was appointed assistant principal. That year he also started, workshopped, and executed a summer program for at-risk youth from the neighborhood based on the concept that if you teach skills like focus, commitment, and vocational skills, you will help students with self-esteem.

At age twenty-nine, he applied for a job as the assistant dean at a large private high school with a very good reputation. He beat out all of the competitors for he job. While he was in the process of interviewing from the job, he heard from students on their complaints with the administration. They thought that the principal and the other staff at the school did not hear their communication and didn't pay attention to them. He made this one of his top priorities. In her first few months, he made himself accessible to the students by always leaving his door open and engaging in casual conversation with students. His students developed relationships with him, as he encouraged them and pointed out opportunities for the.

Morty set up a new system of student government that pleased both her staff and the students at the school. He improved on older procedures and pioneer new representation for the students, inviting them to speak at every single superintendent's and principals public meeting. One of his weaknesses is impatience. Rather than waiting for other people to get stuff don for him, Morty took more and more on himself. He eventually became burned-out. After that, Morty learned to pick people she could rely on as support. He eventually achieved an almost legendary reputation as the "coolest" administrator, and his fellow staff respected his work.

Later in his career, Morty moved on, and was appointed the head of a prestigious

The Performer often has special talents, and have an easy time getting things done and being efficient. They have a sense for sizing up tasks and the dynamic of work groups. They often radiate an ease and assurance. This inspires confidence from others. They identify themselves with the group or community in whom they work, and they are talented at keeping a group cohesive. Networking is big for the performer. The have charisma and a face of argument, which can win them great influence and success in work projects and other pursuits.

Type Threes will often have great difficulty in perceiving their own feelings. They are also holding their finger to the wind, like the Giver, but they don't as much as if they are liked or are good, instead they want to know if they are successful, or if they seem like they are winning.

The Performers draw their energy form their successes. They are achievers, careerists, and seek status. The role of achieving protects the three from being able to get to know themselves. They see things as winning and losing.

In childhood, The Performers my have been super- achievers, and heard may people say to them that you can do it! Thais, beneficially, sometimes becomes a self-fulfilling prophecy. Most threes can be optimistic, youthful, intelligent dynamic and productive.

Three's are cool, successful types, they walk through the work seeing what they want and then going to get it. And they do get it, by working hard. They go to great lengths to see that their planes are successful. They want it to look easy and offhand, and don't show how much they are trying for these efforts.

Efficiency is a great value for The Performer. It fits pretty well with the American idea of the American dream: if you work hard enough, you will work you way up. We are all very admiring of the winners in our capital system and don't much like the loser. The threes, when they are living close to the key vice of their personality, are more or less embodying the worst part of the American dream. The root vice here is untruth. They create an image that looks good, and can be sold. You know those Instagram influencers with millions of followers, who spend time carefully crafting their image to further build, their business projects? The Performers.

They don't listen very well, and have the bad habit of filtering out criticism, as they see it as just extra to whatever they are currently trying t o do. They have several plates spinning all the time. They want to know why we are here, what we are doing, and how we are going to accomplish it. They might insist that you are a bore, or they might want to take control of people who they don't find stimulating enough.

One strategy for a Performer to shift into a place of security and growth is to slow down. Simply take time to observe the self and breathe. A Three may find that when they slow down, the feelings that they have been pushing back will raise a little closer to the top. This will allow the Performer to relate to their experience better, and to relate to others. The Performer may not admit it, but they feel overwhelmed a lot.

Type Four is the Romantic.

- Triad: Attacher
- Spiritual Focus: What's missing
- Weakness: Ordinariness
- Strength: Unique creativity, empathy
- Positive Direction: From self-deceit to honesty
- Essence: Universal belonging
- Secure Embodiment: The Perfectionist
- Stress Embodiment: The Giver
- Wings: The Performer and the Investigator

High-Profile Case Example:

C.S. Lewis

C.S. Lewis was an American author and Christian thinker. He was baptized in the Church of Ireland, but reportedly fell away from his faith when he became an adolescent, and came back to the church in his late twenties. Lewis wrote more than 30 books, including the Chronicles of Narnia, and many others about spirituality. You can see in Lewis' work that he was a searcher, and he searched for meaning by creating the art that exists in his books.

Personality Case Example 1

Hazel is an artist, a painter, but she teaches mathematics. She grew up in a rural part of Nebraska, with a family that looked down upon excessive displays of emotion, or any emotion at all. She found out how to control her feelings early on, but they built up, finding a way to get out in her passion for drawing and painting. Her aesthetic achievements and successes were acceptable for her parents: it is alright for a woman to have interests. There was definitely no change that they would support a full-time pursuit of art, however. So she studied mathematics, looking for an abstract way to pursue art while masking it in a scientific field.

As a young woman, Hazel's most meaningful moments were those of beauty and relation, when she experienced someone else receiving her expression kindly. She had a lot of concern, kindness, and spirit to share. Sometimes she might even find that a connection with an animal fulfilled her need to share the beauty of the world.

Hazel lost her mother at the age of eighteen. She felt so much love for her mother, and when she tried to tell her how much love she had as she was dying, her mother had finally been able to accept her expression. She later named her daughter after her mother, and would tell her as a young child how much she loved her mother.

Hazel taught mathematics in a state university with many classes with over thirty students in attendance. The classrooms were old and ill-equipped. Hazel had the chance to be hired at a smaller, more expensive college, but felt that she would have more impact in students' lives at the school where she currently worked. She chose to live and work in one of the most underserved school districts. Sometimes she would work with English-as-second-language students to help them be able to learn in her class. She loves the study of mathematics, and was able to pass on this love and the subject matter in a kind and gentle way. Sometimes the students would act rude and disinterested. Her concern and authentic interest in mathematics as well as their lives helped to develop a good reputation for her at the school. Many students would return to visit Hazel, and she would be heartened to hear of their journeys.

Hazel thinks about her art sometimes, and feels a bittersweet feeling of melancholy. Sometimes she asks, "what if I pursued art fully?" When Hazel turned 45, she rented a small studio space in her town and began to paint again.

Personality Case Example 2

Roger teaches drama in the music program of a prestigious small-town liberal arts college. Growing up, Roger always knew that he loved theater, and spent many years chasing a full-time acting career. He graduated from a great acting program and landed a few parts in off-Broadway shows. After college he got a big break. Roger was cast in a show that had a tremendous amount of media buzz around it, and he knew that this was the production that could've launched him to the next level of his craft. However, Roger quit the production a couple weeks before opening night. Everyone said he was crazy. This had been a huge opportunity and he had been working on if for so long. It was self-sabotage, they said. Roger just shrugged off their concerns. He said he know it was coming, because tin life, the glass was always half empty. Roger had been told by his acting teachers in high school that he could do anything that he set his mind to. He was talented enough to rise to the highest level of professionalism. Roger realized how significant this early teacher was, and the connection that they had had kept him motivated for many years. He wanted to be like his teacher, to have meaning in his life. Roger decided to go back to school and become a drama teacher.

He acme a very sought-after instructor. Sometimes, his passion was so intense that he provoked controversy. He had a unique love of literature and a respect for the level of craft that it required. He also was good at working with the performing arts students. It seemed that you hadn't had the real university acting student's experience unless you had taken one of Roger's classes. A student would come in and experience the rigor, the depth, and the demanding nature of his classes, and be hooked. He had a high quality connection with his students.

The program grew under Roger's influence, and came to have a significant reputation as a leading acting school in the nation. Now, Roger has taught there for about eighteen years, and he is a legend among the students. Older students will introduce freshman to his classes, their recommendation ringing true as the new student becomes enamored with Roger's teaching style. He always has black pants, a black shirt, and some kind of creatively colored scarf on. He has bright blond hair that he keeps long, and looks like some kind of rock star. His celebrity on campus grew and grew as he took some minor roles in independent films over the years.

The Romantic is driven by the need to be special. They put their talents to work to awaken themselves and others to the beauty that is around them in their world. They often express their feelings in art, dance, music, acting, or literature. The y are deeply attracted to things that have a vital energy. They grasp the moods and feelings of other people and the atmosphere of places and events with precision. They are spiritual people they understand the connector of the sacred and profane. They love the realm of the unconscious, of symbols and dreams, and may prefer this world to the real world. Symbols help them to make sense of the world and to express themselves. They have a gift of helping others to develop and appreciation for beauty and art the ritual is important to the four. They

Also Draw their energy from others. The are asking the question to the world "Day you notice me? DO I catch your eye? They strive for aesthetic accomplishment, to be exceptional, creative, esoteric, eccentric, or exotic.

The Drawback to the spontaneity and creativity of a Romantic is that they may become artificial, in a certain sense. This can sometimes be similar to the Performer, in that they want others' perception of them to be nice and neat and perfect, in this case perfectly imperfect. They believe that the world will be saved by beauty.

In childhood, the Romantic often had the experience of meaninglessness and unbearable emotionality. Sometimes sits related to the experience of a loss, sometimes this can be a real material loss such an as detach or grave catastrophe, or it could have been felt emotionally. Positive ole models may have been missing in this upbringing. The child in the search for identity turns toward the inner world, because ether original source for love end affection was missing or was too wear.

The Romantic will sometimes find they directing anger over a loss towards themselves. They believe that they are guilty and "bad". Shame is a common vice for The Romantic. They will find themselves over and over again stuck in situations which are not good for the. They will cultivate their "badness" in this way and therefore will keep perpetuating the behavior.

The Romantic tends to not think much of the norms of society, for the boring, everyday rules of society. They feel themselves to be strangers or outsiders. This gives them an elitist consciousness, which helps them to be mindful of justice.

A Romantic will sometimes fall into the trap of thinking that their longing will eventually result in some ultimate object of their desire being conquered ad taken in, resulting in them being finally happy. They learn along the way that as soon as they possess the object of their desires (whether it be a relationship, job, or material goods) they will immediately be dissatisfied, as their longing becomes centered around a new ideal good.

The Romantic revere great figures like important writers, musicians, or gurus, who have something deep within them to express to the world. They dislike things that are bland, stale, or average. However, they may be simultaneously romanticizing the "unwashed masses" and may have idealized versions of the movements they are not a part of. This is a tendency, which Romantics should be aware of. It can lead to disconnection, an ivory tower-style attitude, and a distance from authenticity.

The key vice for The Romantic is envy. They see people around them with more talent, status, capabilities, or eccentricities than they do, and they can't accept their place in the world. They may find themselves wondering how other people can be happy. They avoid ordinary things. Things that are conventional and normal evoke disgust.

Depression can see itself manifested at a significant rate with The Romantic, as they live in a sweet melancholy sadness that can take their life over. The Romantic who finds themselves trapped in their sweet sadness can find a tat it becomes a fog that pervades life in a very disruptive way. For Romantics, death is something that they consider at length.

Fours need friends and partners who will bear with them without letting themselves be drawn into the mood shifts that fours have.

They takes their feelings very seriously and fare offended when they are hurt.

For a Type Four, the shift into growth of energy and security will involve the Four feeling a new sense of moral compass, a new reality outside of themselves. This may manifest itself in new relationships, moving out of town, or finding another way to have a shift of perspective. The Romantic does this to clear the mind and find new meaning in their situation.

Type Five is the Investigator.

- Triad: Detacher
- Spiritual Focus: Gaining Knowledge
- Weakness: connection
- Strength: Rationality
- Positive Direction: From hoarding to allowing
- Essence: Awareness
- Secure Embodiment: The Protector
- Stress Embodiment: The Enthusiast
- Wings: The Loyalist and the Romantic

High-Profile Case Example:

Albert Einstein

Albert Einstien was a German-born scientist and physicist who developed on of the most important concepts in modern physics. His work also had a huge effect on the philosophy of science which we now take as fact. His work developing the theory of relativity rocked the world. Einstein is a great example of the Investigator, because nearly everyone understands that in order to make such an accomplishment, he had to use his powers of investigation. Clearly, Einstein was a person who asked questions.

Personality Case Example 1

James is a retail store manager. He has a problem of connection. He can be a very effective manager when he is in his element. He feels passionate about his responsibilities in the store. He feels great bringing his work environment into a place of positivity, efficiency, and productivity. However, his subordinates often report that he is not passionate or responsive in the job, and that there is a lack of interaction. James does not see this at first, that he keeps his feelings and thoughts tucked away in secret. He always tried to keep an air of objectivity, to the point where people never knew his real feelings. He didn't want to show enthusiasm for one idea, for the risk of making other employees think

71

that they didn't deserve praise, and was too careful to not criticize misguided ideas.

James places I high importance on nonattachment. He tires to not let feelings mess with his judgment. So when you employees come in to his office crying, why is it difficult for him not to become impatient and cynical? James doesn't think that verbal report is as reliable as written thoughts, and he has a problem providing helpful feedback, like a causal "nice job," and never gets too happy about his business' success.

James sometimes speaks in a monotone when addressing his employees and likes leaving long silences when employees can't come up with explanations. He would rather connect with people by finding solutions together.

Eventually, with some introspection and counseling, James starts to be able to be himself a little more around his employees. James learns to not be so sarcastic and "objective", and start to feel less like a fish out of water. He starts to express his excitement for the work place, and starts to make connections with employees. One employee even excels in the job to the extent that they are promoted and leave for a higher position.

James has a passionate side, and loves to spend time hunting in the mountains on the weekend. This brings him peace and calm as he is methodically doing work that he enjoys, work that involves a lot of observing and investigating.

Personality Case Example 2

Father Robert is the directing priest for his diocese in Ohio. The cathedral at which he works is seventy-five years old, and is known as one of the oldest structures of its kind in the Midwest. He heads the organization that is responsible for 100 clergymen. They range in age from a few new priests in their twenties to a lot in their fifties and up. Robert is nearing the age of retirement himself, and spent only a few years preaching early in his career before he was chosen for larger duties at the diocese after five years on the job. He has a distinct ability to work with people as a preacher and also an administrator. He makes detailed memos and keeps a macro-vision of the needs of the church, and has a great leadership style that makes him an asset to his diocese.

He is a tall man, and his aura matches his physical presence. When Robert walks into a room, people notice. He is a historian in some ways; he has researched many methodologies and lines of inquiry in regard to biblical interpretations and as a counselor to the people. He is an avid seeker of truth and meaning. He has a deep sense of humble quietness to his spirituality. He is beloved by the congregation.

In fact, Father Robert knows the names of most of the congregation. He always tires to meet new church members and keep up his relationship with older members of the congregation. He likes to talk with people, eat with them in the church community center, and help teach Sunday school classes. He says the innocence and spontaneity of the children rejuvenates the energy of the church.

Robert has to work hard to develop interpersonal skills that allow him to handle difficult pressing issues of anxious parents or stressed out member of his church. He his independent minded and he stays aware of the drain on energy that it takes to practice the diplomacy that he employs in his organizations. Sometimes, when his over worked, he finds himself becoming detached from the situations. He sees himself just going through the motions. If he could, Robert would prefer to just communicate through written notes and email. He likes to protect his time and believe that time is of the essence. Minimal emotionality translates in to rational thinking, Robert believes. He thinks that his greatest achievement is being a rational thinking.

Father Robert was one of the first priest leaders in the nation to see the potential for technology to change the way that the administrative duties of the church work. He was the first to buy an early Mac computer, and later, had Wi-Fi in the church before most businesses did. He runs a newsletter for the congregation. He has people from the community write articles and include news about the church. He likes the feeling of being on the cutting edge of technology. He thinks that you have to have an open mind to deal with the chaos of the world.

The investigator is driven by the need to perceive. They are heady people. They think before they act and they act according to objective information. They can be quit open and vulnerable and receptive to new information. They are researchers, inventors, journalists, and explorers. They can be very original and provocative, and tend to surprise people. They are good listeners, active listeners who pay attention. They help others to become more perceptive.

In childhood, The Investigator often experienced extremes in the unbalance of intimacy. It can be augmented by an experience of too much intimacy, i.e. a cramped, non – private living situation, or by a lack of intimacy, where the child received little tenderness and affection. When this happens, children lose the capacity to develop the skills to show their feelings or express them psychically. They sense emptiness in themselves. It is causes by a lack of security and the felling of being unmoored.

The Investigator has some quality's that are somewhat opposite to the Giver. The investigator is a taker. Alas opposed to The Giver, The Investigator is obsessed with taking. They have a passion for collecting, which can manifest itself in thoughts, or the physical practice of collecting or even hoarding.

The Investigator is obsessed with concentrating on seeing everything, absorbing it like a sponge, they are ascetics and librarians. They may be photographers or scientists, trying to take in tall the world around them and make sense of it. They don't like feelings and band subjective talk and fuss. They enjoy precision, being able to maintain calm, at least externally, and keep their feelings sublimated. They often experience difficulties in relationships realign to people close to them. They are good at cherishing the abstract idea of a person, thinking of them in their faraway, abstract version, but cant' deal wit the messy truths of actually being with people.

The investigator should be wary of the tendency to be afraid of intimacy and avoid it with passion. They generally want to be outside of the messy circle of human relationships. They might find themselves as the mystic monk living in a cave, or in a shack out in the woods. They want to avoid attention, ad be the neutral intake monitor of information. That's not how live works. They could think of nothing more beautiful than to sit and look at something, or nothing at all.

There is the downfall here, of course, of being completely overpowered by what you've convinced yourself is "logic". They have what they believe as an understanding of the world. What they don't understand, they don' mess with. The key vice here is knowledge. For these types, knowledge is power. The investigator has a belief that that they can be safe in their lives by having information and details about the world around them. By being informed by the world is never sufficient, as one finds that they music participate in the world, to really live in it.

They might use withdrawal as a defense mechanism. They are afraid of nothing so much as emotional engagement.

We can see here the deep unresolved problem is the love of sefl. They fear that if they are vulnerable to the world, they will be destroyed. perhaps they were taught this in their upbringing; it is not so hard to imagine. This lesson to never be vulnerable can be a powerful, if maladaptive coping mechanism to deal with problems. They want to avoid emptiness.

The Investigator will have to learn to feel secure somewhat if they are to embody their secure self. They might experience the energy for this as a physical manifestation, as Fives are very visceral and can trust their gut instinct. They often feel rushes of energy. If the Five can learn to trust and learn from their physical instincts, they will find themselves better adapted to deal with challenges.

Type Six is the Loyalist.

- Triad: Detacher
- Spiritual Focus: Scanning to seek certainty
- Weakness: Deviance, being seen as different
- Strength: Sound logic, clear thinking
- Positive Direction: From self-deceit to honesty
- Essence: Faith
- Secure Embodiment: The Peacemaker
- Stress Embodiment: The Performer
- Wings: The Enthusiast and the Investigator

High-Profile Case Example:

J.R.R. Tolkien

J.R.R. Tolkien is best known as the author of Lord of the Rings, a phenomenally popular book series which was made into an equally popular film series. Tolkien was actually a friend of C.S. Lewis', and they regularly had conversations about faith. Lewis reports that it was this friendship that helped him into becoming a man of faith again. Tolkien was obviously creative, but one of his identifying characteristics, as reported from those who knew him, was that he was an excellent friend.

Personality Case Example 1

Tina works at a well-respected law office. She has a side-consulting practice, but her main job is as a public defender. She has written about law and has been published in law journals. Tina loves taking on a new, case, standing in front of the crowd in a courtroom and presenting the case. This was not always what she enjoyed. In her first case in her first year of working as a lawyer she was faced with a room full of her peers, and he was so afraid of the situation that she nearly gave up and quit.

She later found herself hiving herself a pep talk. She told herself, you invested way too much time, energy, and work in this career to give up. It's too late to change your mind and this is what you want. She spends the night reviewing her notes, checking for any vulnerability. Once she completed her processes of review, she convinced herself that the argument was as strong as it could've been. Nothing could go wrong. The next day, she woke up, performed well at the trial, and the next day, she woke up and did it again. Slowly, she became more easily able to get up in front of the courtroom, but she never forgot that initial feeling of panic that she felt on that first day.

Over the years, Tina's lectures became well-known for their theoretical rigor. She inspired the staff of the courtroom to think with equal rigor. This was her goal for being a lawyer: to teach people, to be rock solid for her clients.

In her lat e forties now, she has been in her position for decades, and has been offered various administrative duties, but has stayed in the gritty arena of public defender. She is loyal to the practice and despite her desire to move up the chain, she likes her responsibilities as they are. She is a cautious woman, and she engages gently with others who want to rush through task with ill-conceived plans or positions. This has made her an extremely valued lawyer. She e has begun to take on more and more important influence.

Tina has wound down her career as she grows into her fifties. She takes on fewer jobs, and starts to be a more supportive person with law students who come to learn and creates safe spaces for them as they pursue the field she has excelled in.

Tina knows that she is a successful professional, but she also feels that at any moment the universe could pull out the floor from her feet, and that when crises happen, she with feel that old familiar panic. She relies on the energy rush that she gets in intense situations so she knows that she can cope with crisis.

Personality Case Example 2

Patrick is a mesmerizing singer. There is no song that he cannot express with his powerful voice. He doesn't mess around with stage antics or ice=breaking. He just gets on the stage and sings. He doesn't move around a lot when his on stage, and soon the audience is drawn into his body of work that becomes as real as the bodies around them. His tone and dexterity and expressiveness build into the experience of a truly enlightened musician.

Patrick often has a sarcastic and caustic sense of humor, and knows how to employ it to the benefit of the situation. He spent years studying the voice and submerged in the exercises, health practices, and studying that music requires. He has spent time studying music theory, world musics, music history, and instrument theory. He also works as a vocal coach.

However, Patrick is at his best when he is on a stage with a microphone. It provides him with the artistic license to share his experiences with the world. Away from the protection of the stage, he might be known to people as crabby and paranoid. Thos who seek him as a teacher are often a little off put by the sharp questions and intense exercise that he puts them through. He's not as comfortable as a teacher as he is as a performer. He has a bit of a mental block with this; he thinks if he can't teach himself, he cannot see how he could teach anyone else. He is an individualist, and doesn't enjoy working in groups that are too big, for fear of losing control of the group. He is very easily pissed off by what he sees as laziness or unreliability in other musicians. He is no longer allowed to gig with one of the bands that used to be a consistent job for him. He knows this, and he is fine with it. He has a faith in music and for performing.

He lives in what would be called a somewhat sheltered existence. His apartment is a large loft-style abode near the music district of the city in which he lives, and this is where he does all of his communications via phone and email booking gigs, contacting musicians, and practicing. He has a large extended family and they know him as loving, caring, funny and he has a few friends, but not really close ones. He thinks that people are always trying to take advantage of him.

Patrick is driven by energy to drive him toward what interests him, talking whatever problem comes. There are a lot of problems out there in the world, so he stays pretty busy.

The energy he gets from this lets him to keep his career up, earn enough money to stay afloat, and keep moving all the time.

These types are driven by the need for security and certainty. They are very cooperative. They are reliable team players. In relationships, one can always count on their fidelity. Their platonic relationships are often marked b warm hearted and deep feelings. They are often highly original and witty; sometimes they have a grotesque sense of humor. The Loyalist who has adjusted well to their role in adulthood knows how to participate in important traditions with the readiness to take on new paths. They know what is possible and what isn't. In they can help you find the weak points in your project.

Some say that the Loyalist is one of the most frequently encountered personality types

The key vice for Type Sixes is fear and deceit.

They succumb easily to self-doubt. This makes them cautious, and if overtaken by this, they become fearful and have a hard time trusting people. They cense danger in almost every situation. In their worst form, they become victims to their paranoia.

In childhood, you may find that a Loyalist was exposed to many anxieties and dangers, and saw them as such. There is a sense of primal trust that must be developed in early childhood. Some Loyalists report that they could never get to that place with their parents because they were unpredictable, or violent, or cold. As a coping mechanism, these children either look for a protector who they can trust or they learn to detect the slightest signs of approaching danger so that they could keep themselves anticipate what was going to happen.

In adulthood without adjustment this may turn into the attitude that the world ids dangerous, and you always have to be looking over your shoulder. They may feel that they cannot keep themselves safe, and that they need others to keep them safe.

Similarly to Type whatever, they are emotionally dependent on others, and don't reveal a lot about themselves.

The Loyalist might find the unhealthy tendency to want everything to be black and white. They don't want to deal with gray shadows and impenetrable fog. Sometimes they may be predisposed to political fervor, thinking that if they align themselves ideologically with one tradition, they will find security in it.

The Loyalist will face great obstacles to becoming a whole and independent person. At junctures of change in life, such as starting a new job, moving away from home, or other major changes, they might find themselves paralyzed. They could scrutinize every detail and eliminate all contradictions to their own way, losing the important perspective that family and friends provide.

They are pessimists, and anxious about their own success. Being independent and successful will scare a loyalist. The Loyalist is a "loser", and will prescribe that label on themselves and believe it. They participate in self-fulfilling prophecies about their failure in all realms of life. They have a hard time accepting praise.

The downfall of the Loyalist is their continual striving for security.

The defense mechanism for sixes is projection. They often have an imagination for scenarios of apocalyptic terror and often anticipate the worst.

In order to manifest a higher stage for themselves, The Six needs to be vulnerable. They must put down the fear of everyone and everything, relax, and understand the unconditional love of another. A Type Six may find that they have a deep insecurity. Whatever it takes to address these insecurities, find it for yourself. It may come from exploring past issues, or it may come from creating art or journaling. The Loyalists will need to be kind to themselves when going through this process.

Type Seven is the Enthusiast.

- Triad: Detacher
- Spiritual Focus: Plans and options
- Weakness: Pain
- Strength: optimism
- Positive Direction: From no limits to restraint
- Essence: Commitment to work
- Secure Embodiment: The Investigator
- Stress Embodiment: The Peacemaker
- Wings: The Protector and the Loyalist

High-Profile Case Example:

Oscar Wilde

Oscar Wilde was an Irish poet and playwright. Wilde wrote in many different formats throughout his life, and is most remembered for his novel "The Picture of Dorian Gray". Wilde is known to have had a limit-pushing lifestyle; he wore his hair long when it was certainly not acceptable, and was known for dressing in a flambouyant manner. Wilde was a true artist and a maximalist.

Karla is a national park ranger at
Olympic National Park. She chose to be a park
ranger because it allowed her the opportunity
to frequently explore nature and be free in the
wild. She likes young people and she takes on
lectures for students who attend at the park.
This gives her a sense of fulfillment and fun.
Karla knows how to keep her work enjoyable.
She travels to conferences for forestry workers
and keeps abreast of the new perspectives in
her field. On the side, she maintains a business
growing vegetables to sell at farmers' markets.

Karla's passion is for travel, and she gets
to travel a lot for her work. She views the
world as her oyster to be traversed on a whim.
Once, she had a love affair with a young man
in the forestry industry in Arizona. She
surprised him by treating him to a three-day
weekend in Las Vegas. The danced, ate and

drank, and seemed extremely compatible at the time. However, Karla soon broke off their relationship at the height of its promise: she felt too young, that she couldn't settle down. Besides, she felt that she might meet many other attractive and compatible people in her life.

Karla had charm and an easygoing way with people, but young people in particular. Students and coworkers alike appreciate her optimism. She has a sense of irreverence rooted in the belief of equality, and can be blunt around people with power or those with less power than her.

Eventually, Karla was offered a higher administrative job at Grand Canyon National Park. She jumped at the opportunity to live in a new place and meet new challenges. She started fantasizing about her life in Arizona much before she actually moved there. Her colleagues and students were surprised to see such a quick change in her life. Karla just took it as the way she was meant to go down on her journey. She isn't afraid of not having a job. She can't see the sense in setting limits for herself. She has faith that her future will turn out nicely.

Personality Case Example 2

Lucius is in his late thirties. He consults for a business firm and has had a varying history in different industries. In college he was very interested by the creative fields, especially connected with literature, and he studied creative writing. He had a rock band, which became somewhat successful and allowed him to tour the country. The and had some money trouble in Colorado, so Lucius worked his way back to New York by taking various jobs, from an office job in an agricultural company, to a rodeo clown, to a waiter in a large city. Lucius is interested by the pathways that connect to make up his life's journey. He has a curiosity about people and a sense of adventure. The lie of freedom, life on the road, these notions really spoke to Lucius.

He achieved his undergraduate degree and went on to study Semiotics in graduate school. He chose to work in Semiotics because, as he says, he is loves to be spontaneously intellectual, to be free in his academic pursuits, to let his mind fly into a fantasy world that he could created to appreciate art and literature. His first job as a consultant did not go so well. He was angry to experience the limitations of the business world, and felt like he wasn't experiencing personal growth due to being curtailed by the institutional regulations. He did not see himself as an authority figure.

The concept of a magic circle intrigued Lucius for decade. After he eventually quit his consulting job, he went to the Pyramids of Egypt to experience the immense power of the ancient structures. This started him on a path of travel and study that eventually grew into a performing arts program based on the history and anthropology of the world.

Lucius was able to find foundations to support his work financially, and now runs a non-profit that involves kids in cultural exploration around the history of art. He is hired by organizations around the U.S. that focus on integrating cultural experiences in schools and has spearheaded many new programs to increase arts in education.

They are driven by the need to avoid pain. They are radiant, optimistic, and very alive. They are very mindful people. They can feel childlike in moments when others have difficulty. They have immediacy to their spirit. They are full of idealism and plans for the future; they can pass on their enthusiasm to others. They are cheerful and love to be with people and children.

In childhood, the Enthusiast may have experienced an event that they felt was too much to hold, and to avoid the repetition of similar event in the future, they may evolve to repress their original negative experience. Many Enthusiasts paint their story in a positive light; suggesting that you cant let it get you down.

Have you heard that song Tracks of my Tears? That's about an Enthusiast. Smokey Robinson sings, "Take a good look at my face. You'll see my smile looks out of place. Look a little bit closer and it's easy to trace the tracks of my tears". It is the Enthusiast that has this permanent smile. The Enthusiast is the "eternal child". They are curious and need change, stimulation and new environments and experiences. They have a calendar full of beautiful and exiting obligations.

The Enthusiast finds that procrastination and avoidance cause trouble in their life. Unpleasant tasks are thrust aside, put off, or ignored.

The key vice for sevens is idealism, of a certain kind. They must be sure that they are working for a good cause. One result of this is that they deny and repress aspects of their activity that could have the slightest chance of hurting other people. This obviously leads to clashes between their needs and the needs of other people.

The Enthusiast who has shifted into a growth pattern will find that they relish privacy. Their mind doesn't slow down, and they like to be free to do their mental gymnastics on their own. A well-adjusted

Enthusiast, however, will be able to balance the need for this personal leisure with other parts of life.

Type Eight is the Protector.

- Triad: Defender
- Spiritual Focus: Power and control
- Weakness: Vulnerability
- Strength: Empowering others
- Positive Direction: From excess to trusting sufficiency
- Essence: Truth
- Secure Embodiment: The Giver
- Stress Embodiment: The Investigator
- Wings: The Enthusiast and the Peacemaker

High-Profile Case Example:

Dr. Phil

Regardless of his medical certifications, Dr. Phil has made a name and a career for himself out of being in the role of a protector. Dr. Phil is a TV presenter who created a program where he was able to help people stand up to their family members, friends, or whomever else needed standing up to.

Personality Case Example 1

Martin found himself in an unbearable situation. He wanted to find a place where he could be an educator, but he simply could not put up with the public school system. There was too much regulation, all to protect the power of the authority, and it was hard to get past these and get into the cause of learning. He hated the small-mindedness that he found in the public school system.

However, his students in his middle-school classroom saw quite a different side of martin. He had a great ability and passion for helping them to learn. This was his element, his territory, and he made the rules. Martin believes that education is about giving empowerment to young people. Truth and fairness is a big deal in Martin's classroom. Each year, the students would come in, and Martin would instruct them to put into words their commitment to keeping the class a safe place for everyone, to abide by the rules, do homework on time, and support the classroom environment. Martin had a policy of how to deal with situations in which a student was not honoring this commitment. His policy was thus: when a student broke the roles, he or she had to tell the class what if felt like to mess up. The other students told the student who had broken the rules how if felt to be in the room with them breaking the rules. Martin saw this as a way to engender justice in the kids. The issues of morality in the classroom were often black and white. He put people on the spot to help them to speak for themselves. The lesson that he wanted to impart was truth, and he believed that truth was the way to empowerment. Martin's classroom did provide challenges to the students. Some of the m had a hard time dealing with the string, forceful nature of the culture in the classroom. However, Martin's supervisors support him.

Martin continued to try to take on the school system mano-y-mano, but eventually saw himself being outpaced by the regulations and bureaucracy of the school system.

Suddenly one year, Martin resigned. He felt sad about abounding the current cohort of students, but he rationalized that they would have an effective teacher with or without him.

After he had resigned, Martin became aware of a private school in town. He became interested in working they're, thinking that he might find a better environment for his personality. One day, he marched into the office of the school president and asked if hi could head the special education department. He got the job and learned to love helping the underdogs in the system This proved a great feat of accomplishment for Martin, and he felt much more at home and free in his new position.

Alyssa is an attractive woman, lean, of medium height, and she has a tremendous presence. You can feel her assertive, almost belligerent energy preceding her as she approaches. She's been working as an auto mechanic for almost twenty years, though you'd never know it by looking at her. She had taken a couple of breaks, working various jobs, but always came back to the same old garage. When asked why she came back, she barks out her answer: "I like this place. I like the neighborhood. I like cars."

Alyssa always wears the same overall outfit, and she is a passionate worker. She has an intellectual power to diagnose and find solutions to mechanical problems. She leads her team of mechanics forward in a battle to victory over the body of work that they have to conger. Her vocabulary takes on a sort of militaristic bent. She plans a campaign, wages war, doesn't take prisoners when there are only a few hours left in the day.

Alyssa is tough, and finds herself often berating the young generation, which she labels the "screen generation". She finds that they are always looking at a screen, letting life pass them by. She leads a battle in her own life against this, not allowing her kids to access screens before the age of 10, and is open when she finds someone being disrespectful by looking at their phone too much in public.

Some people love Alyssa, and some people, not so much. She brings her intellectual energy to every environment she finds herself in. Younger mechanics are extremely impressed by her skills, but at the same time are scared of her prowess and intensity. She has a lot of strong opinions. She will push and challenge a young mechanic, making them work harder than they though they could, as she can see that they will be better mechanics than they themselves can see.

The Eight will impress you as strong and mighty. They have a sense of strength to their spirit and are able to care for and protect others. They instivictively know here something stinks, where injustice or dishonesty is at work. They can be a rock of stability and they take on sometimes incredible amounts of responsibility.

The Eight is an interesting inversion of the One Personality; instead of internalizing the message that they should always strive to "be good", they internalize the message that they need to be "bad", that the world will.

The weak, and that sort of tendencies will only lead to suffering. The childhood of at Protector will often be characterized with repression and being pushed around. They could trust now nobody but themselves.

They have the idea that you can't show weakness or cry. Some eight reported that their parents rewarded strength over other values. They have the voice of " Don't take it! Hit back! Show them whose boss! This is the rule that The Protector abides by: don't back down, don't show weakness. They sometimes are confused for the Perfectionist, but unlike the perfectionist, they are not easily able to admit fault. They developed sterght to resist, to break the rules, and to order others around rather than be a follower themselves.

One positive aspect to this is that the Protector rarely puts up with false authorities or unjust hierarchies. They have a passion for justice and truth. This often leads them to help and side with oppressed people. This is because they know within their innermost self there is an inner child, which is the opposite of the strength that they project to the world. When the Protector is in power themselves, however, their subordinates often feel oppressed, because the Protector is most oriented to protecting themselves.

Different personalities have different ways of making and sustaining human contact. For the Perfectionist, it may be involving people in a project that they are helping to make "perfect". For the Protector, a way of making human contact is actually fighting. It could be called confrontational intimacy. They enjoy struggles and conflict. They don't always understand that not all people enjoy struggle and conflict. They don't notice how aggressive they can be. Conflict is their currency. Jokes may go awry.

They are often competitive and very good at games and sports. They have ability to sense weaknesses of others and they are good at taking advantage of others' weaknesses.

The Protector often has the power to help others reach their potential. This in the case that the Protector is able to harness the virtues that they are gifted with and to control the key vice, which is shamelessness. The protector's actual energy is not anger or rage, while sometimes it can seem that way. It is a passion and total commitment to truth, life, and justice it is a passion for the cause they believe in.

Don't let yourself be intimidated by Type Eights. They may make noise, but their bark is sharper than their bite. They are often described as "larger than life".

The pitfall of the eight is when they get obsessed with revenge and retaliation. They become the self-appointed peoples court to pass judgment on their foes.

Eights must strive for innocence.

The well-adjusted Eight will find themselves shifting to be more vulnerably, needy, and open. They will start taking care of others in a more gentle way, focusing less of confrontation and more on cultivation. They can access their defense mechanisms from here in a safer, more productive way.

Type Nine is the Peacemaker.

- Triad: Defender
- Spiritual Focus: The agenda of others
- Weakness: Conflict
- Strength: Unconditional love
- Positive Direction: From being asleep oneself to the right action
- Essence: Universal love
- Secure Embodiment: The Performer
- Stress Embodiment: The Loyalist
- Wings: The Protector and the Perfectionist.

High-Profile Case Example:

Carl Rogers

Carl Jung was a very notable psychologist who made the concept of humanistic psychology much more widespread. Rogers invented the idea of unconditional positive regard. Unconditional positive regard is the idea that when you meet someone, you show them love, no matter what they show you. This concept is elemental to modern psychology and it is useful for anyone wanting to connect with others in a meaningful way.

Personality Example 1

Breanna is the assistant to the director of her mid-sized city's philharmonic orchestra. She is in charge of many aspects of the orchestra's production, from program design, to production management, to green room preparations. She also has a wonderful sense of musicality and is a violinist herself. She is thirty-one years old, and is a loved figure in her community. All different staff workers associated with the orchestra appreciates her warmth, her support, and her enthusiasm.

Breanna has a music room at home, and it is a sty. She has assortment of old programs, sheet music, orchestra posters, and the room is dusty. She has some pieces of stage memorabilia here and there – a signed piece of sheet music from a famous cellist's folder is framed on the wall – and a cosmetically rough piano sits in the corner, piled high with stacks of papers. Music constantly spills from a speaker, the source of which is unknown. Breanna has a special place on her desk that is devoted to her husband and three small children.

Breanna makes it clear that she is causal and fun at work. She makes jokes, pokes fun at the players, and generally makes sure that they are having a good time with each other. To an outsider, her workplace looks extreme and chaotic, but it's a controlled chaos, and Breanna insists that she can't do her job without being chaotic in her office. She plays fast and loose with deadlines and rules, but manages to handle responsibilities, albeit in a messy way.

She is aware of her issues with organization. She tries sometimes to fix things up and keep them in order, but nothing ever seems to change. Sometimes, when Breanna gets overwhelmed, she might start blaming others when it is unreasonable. Eventually, Breanna got her own assistant, and was able to bring more organization and order to her work and life.

Personality Example 2

Max is the director of a large non-profit that is based in Chicago. The organization coordinates funding for various programs that provide education to underserved populations. Max worked for years at a local university and rose through the ranks, becoming an assistant dean. Eventually, he started the non-profit with his friend and established it as a working organization.

Max is a single father to two children, one of which is now working after graduating from college. The other is about to leave home for school. Max and his wife split up years ago; she cited his passivity as one of the major factors for their troubles.

Max is an effective worker and is known as a great father. He also cares for people outside of his family. People know him as a person who they can tell their troubles to. He goes to great lengths to help people. He's a good cook and enjoys being the guy people can rely on at a barbeque. Max tends to function by gaining energy by being around other people. People like to come to his home, which feels very comfortable. It is an interesting home, but you don't feel like you have to walk on eggshells there. There are a few pets around, all adopted.

Max's business partner really values his support, and he works well with Max. He has learned when to give Max the lead and when he needs to fill in Max's weak spots on projects and coordination. Max has proven in his leading of the non-profit that he is an excellent mediator. When there is a discussion to be had with an administrator, donor, or other business entity, he is able to use his instincts to adapt his communication and create agreements. He makes people in the group feel that he is trying to get everybody together to benefit the whole community, rather than getting stuck in petty or unnecessarily tedious issues. He has a warm, vulnerable disposition.

Max finds that he is mostly content in his life. He feels that if he sticks to what he knows, life will work out. Things have gotten fairly stable and ordinary t this point, and Max is comfortable with that. However, Max sometimes finds that he feels lonely, and feels a little resentment that he does so much and doesn't feel that others do the same for him.

Max doesn't like thinking about that, and he tunes it out by listening to a 70's rock n roll record or watching a good movie.

The Peacemaker is driven by the need to avoid. They have a gift of acceptance for others. They don't approach others with prejudice and they make people felt understood and accepted. They can be very unbiased, because they have a sense of kindness around vice. They express harsh truths very calmly and are able to handle matters of deep emotionality with power and grace.

It is arguable that the Peacemaker is a sort of default personality for humans, unaffected by the lack of skill or love from one's parents. If we hadn't grown up in whatever context we did, in such a technologically developed item, we may all be type nines.

With all their abilities for peace and kindness, the Peacemaker may have a hard time understanding their own needs and their own nature. They need to find out what they actually want, who they are, and how they can exist in the world.

Sometimes the Peacemaker's problem is that they lack courage, or don't have enough of a sense of self that they find themselves important enough to show their talents to other people. They can fade themselves in and out of everything and be everywhere but nowhere. If sometime else broaches a subject, they take it up, though not necessarily with great passion, if their partner changes the subject, they address that. They like to swim with the current.

In childhood, the peacemaker may find they were either overlooked or swamped. They were ignored or rejected if they expressed their own opinion. The interests of their family were more important than theirs. There is a collectives bent to this personality type. Peacemakers found themselves as children in such difficult situation that they had to find the reasonable middle ground as a child and see both sides, before they were truly mature enough to do so.

The Peacemaker is lovable. They are so charming and elastic. They like to take the path of least resistance and might be afraid of decisions that will pin them down into any specificity. The key vice of the Peacemaker is belittling themselves.

To ascend in his or her development, the Peacemaker must learn to access energy and drive to achieve goals, and the ability to organize and engage. They can usually stay away from competitiveness or unrealistic expectations. The way that a Peacemaker can go off the rails is by completely losing themselves in their vision of the world. The Peacemaker must remember that they themselves can enact change. When The Peacemaker is feeling depressed, they must remind themselves that inaction will feed their lack of motivation.

Chapter : 3
Learning To Type Others

The teachings of G.I. Gurdjieff and Oscar Ichazo have much to do with the Enneagram gaining as much prominence as it has in recent decades. Ichazo and Gurdjieff were teaching far away from each other, using different methods and languages, but their common interest of helping people to become their deepest authentic selves through a program of inner work. Gurdjieff worked and lived in Russia and then France. Ichazo established a school in Arica, Chile in the 1960's, where he taught his way of using the Enneagram for self-analysis.

Gurdjieff was the one who connected a Platonic-inflected conception of essence versus form in his teachings. He taught that one had both an essence and a personality. The essence of a person is their nature; it is some inherent truth of their being. It is the nature of a person. The personality is what has arisen from the context and circumstances that we grow up and develop with. The way to finding one's essential self, to Gurdjieff, was spending time in a rigorous program of observing oneself, and that we all individually and collectively need to strive for transformation to evolve.

Oscar Ichazo is largely responsible for the Enneagram system of personality that most people work with today. Ichazo initially labeled the system of self-analysis used to work with the Enneagram as "protoanalysis". He had one particularly bright student named Claudio Naranjo. Naranjo studied with Ichazo and he carried over Ichazo's teachings to Berkeley, California in the early 70's. Naranjo led groups of people participating in protoanalysis, and taught about the personality types. Naranjo was born in Chile but had trained in the United States as a psychiatrist. He took many different perspectives into consideration in his development and teachings, including Jungian archetypes, the work of Karen Horney, existential philosophy, psychoanalysis, and the work of G.I. Gurdjieff. The Enneagram struck him as a powerful tool for personal growth and an integrative model of personality.

The teachings of Gurdjieff, Ichazo, and Naranjo fall into several different categories of study. Some have suggested the term "psychospiritual", that is, addressing problems of both psychology and spirituality. When we compare the psycho-spiritual system of teachings presented by Gurdjieff, Ichazo, and Naranjo to psychoanalysis, we see a great number of similarities. Both theories of the Enneagram and psychoanalytic theory view personality as a result of the interaction of a child with the world. They both want to take into account the child's innate disposition and the child's environment. One difference is that psychoanalytic theory focuses a little more on childhood, and the Enneagram is applicable equally to children and adults.

Fr. Richard Rohr is an American Franciscan friar who was ordained into the priesthood in 1970. Rohr is partly responsible for framing the Enneagram and its wisdom into a Christian perspective. He wrote a book in 1995 which brought the Enneagram into the spotlight for many Catholics. At this time, the Enneagram was introduced to a wider audience as a tool for spirituality.

There is a holistic quality to the Enneagram system of personality. It directs our attention to the tripartheid division that we all experience in the head, head, the heart, and the body. This is mirrored in the intellect, emotion, and behavior. The Enneagram supports an equal consideration of body and mind, as often seen to non-western philosophy. The Enneagram supports a balance of these three for functioning.

When using the Enneagram to distinguish which Type you associate most closely to, you want to consider some different elements of the Enneagram's map of personality. The Enneagram makes some distinctions in categories: the gut, the hart, and the head types. These correlate to sexual drives, social drives, and self-preserving drives.

So what le now, an important part of considering the Enneagram and unlocking these personality types to better understand others and improve communication is that each person is a microcosm of the whole system. That is to say that all nine types think, feel, have a sex drive, a drive for self-perseveration, and social impulses. All nine types have strengths and faults. So in parsing your own type and other personality types, you must remain conscious of the common attitudes that we have, and also the contextual factors for personality. Betty, in the office, may only be showing you one side of her that will lead you to think she's a Protector. But in most of her life, she is the Loyalist. When she is challenged to an extreme, she behaves like The Investigator. We may embody many different aspects of each of the personalities, but if you were able to look closer into Betty's life, you'd see that she has core attitudes and developmental tendencies that align with the drives of one type.

What leads us to our most core personality type? People have to survive in the world! We start to organize traits and characterizes that will let us make our way and form relationships, with others and ourselves. Personality is mad up of our defense mechanisms, habits of thought, the emotions that come with the thoughts, interpersonal aptitudes and abilities, and a way of physicality to manifest our energy. Once we understand our tendency to have one way of living, we can unlock the opportunity for proactive, rather than reactive behavior.

The Triads, wings, and variants of the Enneagram model can provide even further insight into our behaviors and tendencies. Both of the types on either side of any given Enneagram type are the wings of that type. People are never always one of the personalities described in the Enneagram; they are always a combination of one or two of them. This is one reason why no two people ever seem completely alike in their behavior. If an individual is mainly a Type Three, the wings of Type Three will also be present in their behavior and personality. This means that sometimes they may embody the characteristics of a Type Two, and sometimes they may imitate a Type Four. Some will say that an individual draws equally from both wings, that is, if they are a Type One, that they derive equal influence from each of their wings. Others think that people tend to characterize the influence from only one wing at a time.

Let's discuss the secure and stress embodiments of each of the types. The Enneagram's lines illustrate an individual's shift in personality when they are facing security, versus the shift in an individual's personality when they are feeling stressed or disintegrated. Each type has two lines that connect it to other points on the Enneagram. Depending on the type of situation that the person is facing, they tend to adopt or embody the characteristics of a certain other type. Here are the directions of the lines that illustrate the stress embodiment: One shifts to Four, Four shifts to Two, Two moves to Eight, Eight moves to Five, five moves to Seven, and Seven moves to One. Within the triangle, Nine shifts to Six, Six shifts to Three, and Three shifts to Nine. When individuals are feeling safe and secure, and perceive themselves as healthy, there is the secure embodiment. The lines that illustrate the shift to a secure embodiment are such: One shifts to Seven, Seven moves to Five, Five moves to Eight, Eight shifts to Two, Two shifts to Four, and Four shift to One. IN the triangle, Nine moves to Three, Three shifts to Six, and Six shifts to Nine.

Wings of a personality certainly complicate things, but the geometry of the Enneagram is such that it holds a pattern and organization. There are many different ways to look at the Enneagram. It may make sense to consider it a cycle in itself, starting from the Type One, moving to the Type Two, and down along the line. The Type Nine, the Peacemaker, is where the cycle restarts. The Wings for a personality inform and affect the way that the personality is expressed. The Perfectionist, while having a huge drive for perfections, will sometimes find the need to help people as a "perfect" endeavor. This would demonstrate the Type One taking on the characteristics of its wing on that side. The Performer will sometimes find that they want to "perform" as a helper. This would be the Performer's wing of Type Two impacting the Performer. Sometimes the Performer will have an artistic bent, and will take up cello or painting or writing. It's no coincidence that the Performer is situated next to the Romantic, who is desperately in love with all forms of art.

Chapter : 4
Working With Types

If you haven't done so already, you may find it interesting to attempt a self-assessment of Enneagram type. You are probably the only one who can do this classifying for yourself; after all, you know yourself best. First, five yourself some time to study and look at each of the types, so that you can get a good picture of what each of them can look like. There are a few different well-established Enneagram self-report questionnaires. One of them is the Wagner Enneagram Personality Style Scale. Another is the Riso-Hudson Enneagram Type Indicator. Before you take any type of personality inventory, you should make sure it is coming from a trusted source, and has sufficient levels of validity and reliability.

The Enneagram

Discover your type with this quick and easy Enneagram test!

For each question, note a mostly true or mostly false. It doesn't have to be 100% true or false, just what is closer to true or false. You'll need a pencil or pen and a scrap of paper for this test.

There are nine sections. Instructions will follow the test in order to obtain your results.

Section 1

I like rationality and reason.

1. People who don't stick to the rules don't appeal to me.
2. I don't like chaos.
3. I feel that I have a purpose.
4. I like things to be morally defensible, and that is a priority for me.
5. I need to be in control.

6. There is a clear good and bad in the world.

7. I find that I can usually find the truth in a situation.

8. People have described me as idealistic.

9. My life revolves around making things perfect.

Section 2

1. I like to help others

2. I don't like when I am in a leadership role.

3. I find it hard to ask for help.

4. People can trust me.

5. People tend to lean on me.

6. Generosity is a major part of my life.

7. I prefer it when other people are happy with me.

8. I get jealous sometimes.

9. Self-discovery is not that important to me.

10. Helping others is my job.

Section 3

1. I am driven to succeed.

2. I like to win.

3. I can adapt to different situations easily.

4. I worry about what others think of me.

5. Other people often say that I do great things.

6. I am very successful in my work.

7. There are very few situations which vex me.

8. In school, I got very good grades.

9. Helping others is good but not a priority of mine.

10. I try to excel at everything I do.

Section 4

1. Art is what drives me.

2. I tend to be withdrawn.

3. I have been involved in music, dance, or drama.

4. I do a lot of self-reflection.

5. I can get emotional.

6. Meaning is a major drive for me.

7. The world is sometimes overwhelming.

8. I prefer to be alone much of the time.

9. I like to connect with others on a deep level.

10. I love movies.

Section 5

1. People have described me as intense.

2. I like thinking games.

3. I enjoy solving problems.

4. I have innovated new solutions where previously there weren't any.

5. Sometimes I can be secretive.

6. I tend to isolate.

7. Figuring stuff out motivates me.

8. I don't enjoy being the center of attention.

9. Sometimes I act like a detective.

10. I am very observant and perceptive.

Section 6

1. I am a great friend.

2. I don't have any problem committing to things.

3. I like to feel safe and secure.

4. I like to engage in conversation.

5. I am responsible.

6. Others have described me as anxious.

7. I have trouble standing up for myself sometimes.

8. I am a very good team player.

9. I'd rather be in small groups of people.

10. I like being in lasting relationships.

Section 7

1. I like to keep busy.

2. People find that I am entertaining.

3. I love spontaneity.

4. I can do a lot of things.

5. People look to me as a leader.

6. People have described me as scatterbrained.

7. I get distracted easily.

8. Having fun is a priority.

9. I love talking to people.

10. Career goals are not of the utmost importance.

Section 8

1. I am good at competition.

2. I don't like to feel powerless.

3. I like playing sports.

4. I am fairly confident.

5. Making decisions is not hard for me.

6. I have a strong will.

7. I'm not afraid of confrontation.

8. People look to me for protection.

9. I don't mind conflict.

10. I have trouble looking inward at times.

Section 9.

1. People describe me as easygoing.

2. In the past, I have used self-effacing humor.

3. I am a good listener.

4. I am generally a good helper.

5. I like to be in agreement with most people.

6. Sometimes, I get complacent.

7. I have idealistic goals.

8. I find that I am a good leader in certain situations.

9. I don't like conflict.

10. People have called me wise.

Great! You made it to the end of the test. In order to see the Type with which you most closely align, go back and add up how many statements you marked down as true. The category with the most marked true will be the number of the Type that you have associated yourself with the most.

Most of the theory around the development of personality in the Enneagram acknowledges a humanistic viewpoint, influenced by the psychologist Carl Rogers, among others. Humanistic theory suggests that people come up with a set of defense mechanisms and coping strategies to maintain their safety and health in the world. Some of these coping strategies may be healthy, and some may not. This provides the distinction between adaptive coping strategies and maladaptive coping strategies. An adaptive coping strategy is a way that you deal with problems and challenges in the world that is healthy and helpful, without providing a lot of negative side effects. A moderate amount of exercise, expressing emotions through art, or attending therapy groups are examples of adaptive coping skills. Some examples of maladaptive coping skills would be avoidance (staying at home to avoid your problems), drug abuse, or violence.

Whatever coping skills we develop, that becomes a sort of identity in itself, and we start to think of ourselves as identified by those skills. In reality, these skills represent only a part of us, whether they are adaptive or maladaptive, and there is an authentic, ultimate version of us inside ourselves. The Enneagram presents a basic schema by which we can investigate our adaptive and maladaptive coping mechanisms. Often, the Enneagram cannot only tell you about your faults, but also how you are limiting yourself. You might hear a description in the Type that you realize you are not achieving because of some kind of block.

The Enneagram theory can be integrated with western theories of development quite well, and Claudio Naranjo did a lot of this in his work. Naranjo thought that in reaction to pain and anxiety, people seek to cope with an urgent situation with equally urgent coping mechanisms. When the urgent situation or threat is repeated, we find what works best, and we continue to carry out those behaviors. The behaviors become learned and rewarded, and continued into adulthood.

This view is essentially congruent with object relations theory. Object relations theorists believe that the personality comes out of the persons complicated way of adapting to her environment. The individual is striving for instinctual needs, such as the need for relationship. Another instinctual basic need is individuation, or being different and independent enough.

People, as we know, are extremely complicated. Obviously, nobody is perfect there are many parents who meet their children's needs too little, and some too much. As needs become unmet or overgratified, the child develops coping mechanisms. If the situation stays the same for a long time, the behaviors will become fixed. This is what makes up our personality or character. A popular positive psychology adage goes, "Watch what you think, your thoughts become your actions. Watch what you do, your actions become your habits. Watch your habits, your habits become your character."

When this process is enacted, it is almost impossible for a young person to analyze what has happened. The actions and habits become unconscious, and in this, the person becomes unconscious to the fall from consciousness. We start thinking that what we do is just who we are. This is often seen in addictions. The person starts to think, "I am Karen, I drink every night and that's just what I do." You can imagine all sorts of situations where people use this justification to continue with the negative manifestations of their personality. It ultimately results in the person being blocked from accessing their authentic self, and they end up limiting their development into what they potentially could be.

Here's a more thorough description of how this happens:

1. Self-Affirmation: the initial onset of the problem and the expression of need
2. Negative environmental response: the environment's (or parents') rejection of fulfilling that need

3. The Reaction: this is the automatic response to the rejection that has been experienced. It is often a negative emotional experience, ie, rage, terror, or sadness.

4. Self-negation: This step is where a child or person learns to turn against himself or herself. They are now trying to block the initial need that they expressed, learning that their needs cannot be met. They also begin blocking the experience of the negative environmental response. It is and identification with the lacking environment. This is the onset of a potentially life-long conflict, and is where many of our pathologies arise. It is where we learn how to keep ourselves safe by any measure, and often the measures become maladaptive.

5. Adjustment process: This can also be a lifelong process, wherein the person

grows to learn how to compensate for the previous steps, and to become more balanced and make compromises to resolve and unsolvable problem.

Therefore, we are left with our personality. the personality consists of which parts of you have expressed and which parts of you leave repressed. What we are dealing with here is suppression versus exaggeration of our characteristics. With the Enneagram, we get nine descriptions of patterns of thinking, feeling, and acting that get in the way of our essential, authentic selves.

Let's go through the types and explore how the different vices and strengths of each can be caused by or accounted for by adaptive or maladaptive coping mechanisms. At the end of each description, a question is presented. This question may help each of the types to distinguish between their history of adaptive and maladaptive coping mechanisms.

Type One, The Perfectionist, is extremely ethical. They are guided by moralism, and are often teachers or activists. They tend to have a deep fear of being evil or defective. Often the coping skills that The Perfectionist have developed will reflect their wish to be "good", and they may adopt very healthy coping mechanisms early on, such as eating well or exercise. However, there is the risk that The Perfectionist will struggle with setting a balance in these mechanisms, and may struggle with eating disorders or over-exercising. On the other hand, The Perfectionist may sublimate their vice into dark corners that no one gets to hear about, which may involve substance abuse or other ways to blow off steam. When examining how your personality manifests, as a Perfectionist, you should ask yourself, "Why am I trying to be perfect? Who was or is telling me that I need to be perfect? Do I actually need to be perfect?"

The Type Two, or the Giver, is empathetic, genuine, and kind. They are often quite generous and love to help others. The Giver has a fear of being unwanted and not belonging anywhere. This is the drive to feel love. Givers will develop interpersonal ways to protect themselves in the world. They will use relationships to fuel their self-worth. They will often get involved in co-dependent relationships, in which they become dependent on others to be dependent on them. This is an example of a maladaptive coping strategy that The Giver will sometimes take on. If the Giver were able to manifest their personality in a positive and healthy way, that adaptive coping skill would be that they develop intimacy early on, as they have a knack for doing. The Giver should be asking, "Am I sharing enough my weaknesses to the world? Am I allowing myself to be helped?"

Type Three, The Performer, is extremely goal-oriented, ambitious, and charismatic. They are excellent leaders and are driven by self-image and what they perceive others' images to be of them. The Performer was always driven, even at a young age, to do and achieve. This means that they learned early on to be successful, and that that would be what keeps them safe and connected. Success in school and work are certainly protective factors in the life of a child. However, these are the same kids who are pushed by their parents and tried to live up to unrealistic expectations. Resultantly, the kids often lose touch of what is important to them, and find themselves lacking in self-awareness and contentedness. The Performer will find a strong dose of introspection will be helpful early in their journey. The Performer should ask, "Who am I trying to satisfy with my success? Am I truly feeling content with my achievements?"

Type Four is the Romantic. They are dramatic, love expression, creative, and can be self-absorbed. They are careful with their own intimacy, but love diving into creative projects with depth. They are most afraid of not having anything significant about them, of not being unique. They want to establish their identity in the world, and for people to listen to them. The Romantic often learned in early development that they had to find meaning for themselves; they found it hard to connect to what was around them and life felt dull. So they set to work making things magical for themselves. And they usually succeed – even if it has costs along the way. In attending to their creative and artist-selves, they often reject or ignore the practical demands of living in the world. They may be very unorganized. The Romantic, as we know all too well from the biographies of many musicians, artists, and writers, may be predisposed to alcoholism or drug abuse, a maladaptive coping strategy. Their adaptive coping strategies include creating and participating in worlds of art or other aesthetically fulfilling tasks. The Romantics should ask themselves, "Can I admit to myself that I have meaning? Can I admit that I am good and have inherent meaning as a human being?"

Type Five, the Investigator, is typically oriented to be alert and curious they re able to find out why things are the way they are. They are always searching and always asking questions. The Type Five has a deep fear of being useless or incapable. They spend a lot of time looking, listening, seeing, and perceiving the world. The Investigator wants to be protected and empowered by knowing. This is all well and good, but sometimes, what we know can hurt us. The Investigator may have developed coping skills that included gathering information and knowledge to defend themselves from danger. They may have missed out on developing the adaptive skills of drawing boundaries and looking outside their limitations. The Investigator may want to ask of themselves, "What I limiting myself to? Can I accept that there are some things I will never know?"

Type Six, The Loyalist, is extremely committed in relationships and trusts her friends more than anyone. They are very cautions and can be indecisive. The Loyalist wants to guarantee that they will never be abandoned. This is their basic fear – that their support system will up and leave them one day, without explanation. They can worry a whole lot. The Loyalists developed adaptive coping skills for maintaining relationships; they learned how to make friends with people and keep them as friends, by satisfying their needs or keeping them safe. The Type Six feels that enough they have enough support, they will be okay. Type Sixes may learn maladaptive coping strategies, however, that also stem from their type of relationality. They may find that they get in unbalanced relationships, perhaps on the other side of The Giver, and that they find they are needed only to need someone else. In this self-discovery process, the Loyalist should ask them, "Can I be okay with uncertainty? Can I acknowledge the impermanence of life?"

The Type Seven, or the Enthusiast, is always having fun, being spontaneous, and find themselves to have great versatility in social and other situations. They tend to be ever-enthusiastic about the world, wanting to stay busy, and be fulfilled. They have a basic fear of being deprived or being in pain. Almost anything that catches the mind of a Seven will be accepted and taken enthusiastically. They often make the mistake of adopting an attitude of extreme idealism, and become disappointed when the world doesn't live up to their expectations. Their idealism may have bolstered their adaptive coping strategies early on in life; of course, why wouldn't anyone want a friend who is always seeing the bright side and is always available to do that fun thing you planned. The other side of this is that they can get wrapped up in all of these ideas. They may find themselves keeping busy just so they can stay away from exploring their inner life, and they don't actually know what they want. Staying busy to avoid life is a common maladaptive coping strategy in our society. The

Type Seven should ask, "What do I really care about? What am I rationalizing about that is not actually as awesome as I think?"

The Type Eight, or the Protector, is centered on power. They are assertive and strong. They use their resources well and are decisive. Their basic fear is of being harmed or controlled by others. They can also be known as The Challenger; they love a challenge and interacting with others in a competitive way is a strong source of relationality for them. The adaptive coping strategies that The Protector learns to use are usually tied with assertiveness or aggressiveness. Perhaps more than other types, it is easy to see how this behavior can easily manifest in both adaptive or maladaptive coping skills. Of course, if the Protector is in a situation that is dangerous, they will be likely to defend themselves physically. there are other protective factors associated with assertiveness; they may learn to have their needs met easier than less assertive types by being able to demand it. However, the path of assertiveness and the path of aggressiveness are often difficult to distinguish, and it can be difficult to execute one for the Protector without wading into another. The Protector should ask herself, "Is there a part of me that is deeply vulnerable?"

Type Nine is The Peacemaker. The Peacemaker is easygoing, affable, and trusting. They are often creative, can be enthusiastic, and part of support systems. They have a deep fear of loss and separation. They want to have contentment in their souls and others'. They are often "seekers" of spirituality and have a sense of connection to humanity as a whole, not just their particular cohort. The Peacemaker developed coping skills that are centered around making harmony in people and situations. This may have worked out very well for the Peacemaker. If The Peacemaker does not find herself adjusted well as an adult, however, they might find themselves often just "going with the flow", on the one side of a codependent relationship, or just not having their needs met. Their maladaptive strategies may involve being the "yes man" or an enabler. This is where they have found protection. However, as the Peacemaker develops, they learn to have an integrated self, which delineates their own needs as well as the general need for harmony.

The idea of life as a journey is one that permeates all of our historic archetypes and pervades our mythology, literature, and art. Thinking of life as a journey can be helpful in accepting context. Our context is where we are, what we are, how we are, and when we are. For some, the Enneagram is a topic with which they are well familiar. Some people have engaged in self-discovery and analysis for decades before coming across the Enneagram. Where are you in the journey? Whether you are young or old, no matter what resources you have, you are on the journey. This journey, however, is a paradoxical one. There is no beginning and no end. To be striving to find that day where the journey has end is a mistake; this has been found in the Buddhist philosophy. Each day has its challenges and successes, from the first to the last.

If you use the Enneagram to gain insight into your life, you are giving yourself the gift of understanding. To gain understanding is an essential part of being human. Understanding where you are in your journey is important. Be kind to yourself; the voices of judgment may come strongly in some minds; however, the Enneagram is an egalitarian system of categorization. There are not hierarchies, there is no personality that is better than another, and the beginner is just as valid as the guru.

Indeed, we must see the key vice in our personality not only as an evil thing to be avoided and controlled, but rather one to be harnessed and used for good. There is a certain "dissociative" response to vice. We have extreme feelings of shame, guilt, or punishment that reinforce our avoidance of the vices and negative tendencies in our personality. The thing is, our vices have a lot to teach us about ourselves. They tell us about how we defend ourselves, how we relate to others, and how we see the world. The Enneagram invites you into a dialogue with your more negative parts and helps you to see them as part of the whole you. Your creative exploration of the Enneagram should be filled with encouragement and a thirst to become a responsible and whole person.

The Enneagram can be great for multiple people to work on together in small groups. If you are able to find this kind of support system in your Enneagram work, then that's great. Having a small group of people allows you to talk about what you are finding out about yourself and feels safe to explore the shadow sides of our personality. Sometimes others can see you in a different light than you are able to see yourself. They can point out things they've noticed that correlate to Enneagram knowledge, or they can help to clarify your thinking.

Once we can interpret the Enneagram and unlock the meanings of the various personalities and how to interact with them, we are often left with the question of how we go forward and work with the knowledge that we now have. There are many answers to this question. Some of them involve personal dives into the depths of inner self, and involve introspection as the catalyst for and agent of change. This will be easier for some than others, and certainly some will get lost in the depths of their own souls. Introspection can sometimes lead a person to the next step of their development. This can be seen in behavioral changes, such as a young adult who decides to settle their life for the first time. It may be very intertwined with artistic pursuits such as music, visual art, or writing. The journey towards change and self-realization may involve seeing a counselor, religious leader, or family elder for consultation. There are a huge variety of styles of counseling available, from CBT (cognitive behavioral therapy) to hypnotherapists and everything in between.

Whatever the case is for the path taken for change, we now have enough understanding of the brain and its neuroplasticity to know that adaptation in individuals is totally realistic and possible. Neuroplasticity is the brain's ability to create new connection and grow more cells in response to experiences. This ability to grow and adapt at the neuro-psychological level includes both connections that help us to be healthier in life and relationships, and those that don't. This is the where awareness comes in. Self-awareness is understanding our experience of our thoughts and feelings and being able to see when we are acting like a certain type, and when we are embodying the worst tendencies of our type or another's. The Enneagram can help us to use labels and make sense of our personalities, so that we can see our tendencies, and when appropriate, act differently! The Enneagram paradigm allows for deeper understanding, and ultimately, self-acceptance.

The Enneagram is a cosmic symbol, and as such, has different forms and functions. Its geometry is situated in a universally harmonious way, and the geometry of the Enneagram contains a way to map interrelationships that are found in human tendencies and behaviors. One way to use the Enneagram as a map other than a topology for personality which has been developed is a Enneagram for a process of transformation.

The following list is a contextualization of the Enneagram. This one uses the outer circle to describe the temporal events and the inner triangle to denote the phases of inner and outer in our self-development.

Here's how this one is set up:

1. Clarify the problem
2. Plan Initial Strategy and Gather Resources
3. The Value of the Problem Enters
4. Conduct Initial Work to Solve the Problem
5. Find a Way To Solve the Problem
6. Vision of Solution Enters
7. Work Out the Details
8. Present the Results
9. Process Completed/Problem Enters

The outside of the circle illustrates the functional aspects of transformation. It is what goes on during the cognitive tasks we complete regarding problems. Point 0 is when the problem enters our consciousness. We feel attracted to the problem and want to solve it.

This is also the feeling of our previous problems leaving. The circular nature of this problem represents the circular nature of having problems itself!

Point 1 is the task of clarifying the problem. This doesn't always prove to be as easy as it may appear. What exactly and precisely is the problem? Sometimes the problem gets blown out of proportion, or minimized. Let's say that John wants to be more emotionally available. His problem is that he is not sufficiently emotionally available. Or is it? While participating in the type of introspection that is necessary to come across this problem, John may look closer at his problem and realize that he doesn't feel that he personally has enough emotional support. This, rather than the first problem, may become the more important or urgent problem.

Point 2 is to plan and gather. "What are you going to do about that?" This step is a great challenge for some people. For those who suffer with indecisiveness, which can stems from depression, sometimes this is as far as they get. Just try not to decide that you can't do anything about it, because that's not true.

Point 3 is the value of the problem. Sometimes we need to choose our battles. Sometimes the time and effort it takes to solve a problem may necessitate a surrender of sorts. In John's case, realizing that he needs greater emotional support system, that is a very important problem. It is a problem that, if worked on, the working-on will provide the worker-on with many rewards.

Point 4 presents the initial work that is needed to solve a problem. This phase of transformation will be easier if the first few steps are completed successfully. If you are able to make this a straightforward task, it will be easier to complete. Our example case, John, may take this time to start working on establishing connections he has lost, or opening up to others in a mild, moderate way, to get things started.

Point 5 is where one must find a way to solve the problem. This can be a stage of great tension, where the problem is providing enough distress that a threshold for change is met. This stage contains magical moments; John may discover that someone else feels the same way he does, because he put in the work and went to a social event, or he may find he has more courage because of a new connection. This is where we get oriented to the solution.

Point 6 is the vision of the solution. It enters the consciousness and allows us to complete the process of solving the problem. Typically, we start to "get it". I this stage, John is realizing the behaviors that will unlock that social support, and getting better at that. Point 7 is

Point 7 is to point out the details of the solution. What is actually needed to see this thing through? This is where the solution becomes solidified; rather than one instantly it happening, the solution manifests itself over time.

Point 8 is present the results in or put the solution in a form that connects with you. This is to acknowledge that you put in the work to achieve a transformation in your life, and to put it in record so that you can repeat the helpful steps in the future and improve upon your process.

The concepts of awareness, communication, and understanding are all needed to navigate this process successfully. If you don't get caught up in all the emotional and behavioral blocks, these steps can provide a method to responsible deal with difficult situations.

Chapter : 5
Connection and Communication

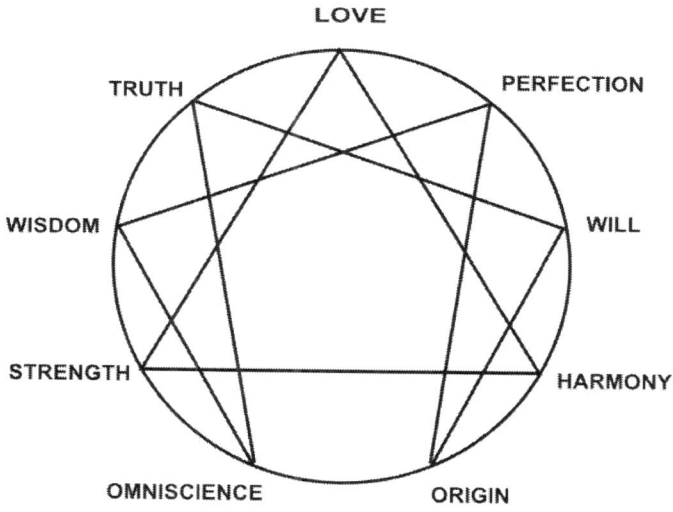

Communication is a very oft-cited problem in relationships. In many different developmental phases, people can find themselves with a low level of self-awareness. The Enneagram can help us increase levels of self-awareness and understanding. It is with this self-awareness and understanding that we can begin to build healthier, better relationships, ones marked by clear and open communication. What gets passed on in this communication is our needs, our goals, and our vision for our lives. The typology of the Enneagram can help us to realize how we are acting and gain insight into our behavior and how we interact with others.

When faced with a struggle of interpersonal dynamics, often we can get caught in a reactive feedback loop. The problem presents: a person becomes annoying, or too needy, or

Here's an example case of how an awareness of your and others' types can lead to a more harmonious work environment.

Katherine works as a full-time university professor, teaching English in multiple classes for college undergraduates. Katherine is a Perfectionist, an Enneagram Type One, and she believes that her strong sense of justice, along with her high expectations and strict standards, have bolstered her ability to be successful in her field. She has recently taken on Sam, a new associate professor, who will be taking on some of the instruction in her classes. Sam is The Enthusiast, an Enneagram Type Seven. Sam took on a great deal of preparation and brought in lesson plans for a month in advance when he started. Katherine was greatly impressed by this, as it shows a high level of expectations and organization. Their initial meeting left them both feeling great about their new work relationship and excited to be working together. They got along quite well, although sometimes Katherine finds that Sam is a little more high-energy and silly in the work environment than she would be. At first, she interprets this silliness as enthusiasm, and sees that Sam is eager to learn and be liked and improve in his work, which she can understand.

As the weeks go on, however, Katherine notices that Sam is starting to sway from staying on track in his classes. He is very smart and competent, but often strays into tangential subjects that get too far away from the class material. Sam has also begun to reschedule their weekly supervision meeting. Katherine has consistently marked in her calendar a day and time to meet, and she wants to stick to that time consistently. Sam reschedules the meeting a couple of times, and Katherine brings up that she wants to have the meeting at the originally scheduled time. Katherine points out that it was their agreement to meet at this time every week, and Sam agrees, but also interjects that they are still meeting every week, just not at that time. "That's not the point", she thinks.

Sam begins to show up at the originally scheduled time for the meeting, and this continues for a few weeks. Then Sam attempts to reschedule the meeting, and Katherine becomes angry, bringing up that it is unprofessional to reschedule meetings at such a high frequency. Sam lets her know that he is very busy and has several projects that he is trying to maintain outside of this job. Katherine dismisses this point outright. Sam walks out of the office feeling misunderstood and bemoaning Katherine's rigidity.

Katherine wonders what to do. She ponders various answers to the situation, and then remembers training in which the Enneagram was used to facilitate understanding of students. She realizes this could be a situation that could greatly benefit from some understanding. She sends Sam the assessment tool for the Enneagram, and asks him to bring it to their next meeting.

When Katherine and Sam meet, they discuss that Sam is The Enthusiast, and to feel happy, he sometimes needs to feel like is busy. He enjoys teaching, and he has the gift for it, but has trouble having the trust in himself to make major commitments like this one requires. He feels that by diving completely into this job as an associate professor, he is missing out on some other opportunities that he might have. He is active in volunteering work, giving some of his time to a local non-profit that works with underserved populations. He is part of a softball team, takes violin lessons, and works out every day. All of these activities have left him feeling tired but fulfilled, and he is exhausted nearly all the time. This is his reason for missing supervision meetings. His intention is not to be disrespectful or unprofessional, but he can't bring himself to drop any of the other activities that he cares so much about. He recognizes, with Katherine in the room, that his spontaneity can sometimes come off as impulsivity and unprofessionalism.

Katherine, the Perfectionist, an Enneagram Type One, tells Sam that she understands that she can be perfectionistic and rigid sometimes, especially when she feels that she is not being respected. She shares with Sam that she has a deep desire to educate, to share her wisdom, and to help young people live better lives. She knows she can be bossy and critical, but it comes from good intentions, the intention of wanting to help others reach their potential. She tells Sam that it is difficult for her sometimes to loosen up and be flexible. She also recognizes the emotions that it brings up in her when people around her do not demonstrate the same adherence to structure.

The two of them sit down and have this conversation, and in the end, they are able to see what each of them need for themselves and need to provide for the other. It is important that Katherine has enough structure to be able to facilitate the type of work environment that she needs. Sam needs some flexibility in scheduling, and they work out a system for when he needs to reschedule; he will let Katherine know enough in advance that it doesn't affect her weekly schedule. They both agree that they will engage in open communication about their needs and obligations. Katherine will try to provide equal amounts of positive feedback and criticism for Sam's teaching, and Sam will create a lesson plan at least a week in advance to be approved by Katherine.

They leave this meeting both feeling understood, connected, and settled with each other. Neither of them tried to change their personality to fit the situation; they both acknowledged aspects of their personality and accepted that they are two different people working together. What they've done is create insight into their situations; Katherine gained some insight about what her personality does to people, and Sam gained some insight into how his life can work better for the people around him. They are establishing a relationship of safety, trust, understanding, and connection.

Katherine and Sam experienced a conflict of personality dynamics in their relationship.

If you examine what happened here, you will find a pretty good set of characteristics that the "intervention", or whatever needs to happen to make a relationship functional again, must have.

One of these is acceptance. There are many people in the world who find in themselves an ability to judge ad then compartmentalize. What does this mean? It means that they have parts of themselves that they have not accepted. It may be an experience that was not able to be integrated, it could be a bad choice they made years ago which affected their life, it could be circumstances outside of their control which they can't accept.

For example, lets take the Type Five, the Observer. The Observer is that smart kid who sits in class and never talks, although you know that he knows most of the answers that the teacher is asking the class. He thinks of the answer, but doesn't say it out loud. Early in childhood, this mostly works; adults can perceive the level of intelligence that these children often have, and they can tell that the child is this type. However, as we develop into young adulthood, we are expected more and more to represent ourselves through our speech and to develop verbal communication in order to be part of the group and develop relationships. There may be a teacher that comes along and says to that kid "You did very well on your written assignments and tests, but I can't give you an A, because you never spoke up once during times of class participation." The Observer will then have to accept this point: that their natural tendency has, thus far, worked, but that they've come to a time when this underdeveloped aspect of their personality must be bolstered and used more. The way to communicate with a Type Five in this situation is like this: you give them a reason. You say, "Hey, you going to have to learn to express yourself, make yourself seen and heard. You have good ides, and you have smart thoughts about the material. I'd love to see you speaking up more." Acknowledge that his abilities are not undervalued.

Let's explore more aspects of Katherine and Sam's way of coming together and communicating using the Enneagram to guide the way. Another thing that they are employing is awareness. Awareness, simply put, is noticing what you are feeling, seeing, hearing, thinking, or doing. Both Katherine and Sam had a level of awareness. Katherine probably has a higher level of awareness, due to her years of experience versus Sam's youth. Katherine was able to use her higher level of awareness to notice her thoughts, feelings, and actions. At first, she noticed that she felt upset when Sam would miss a meeting. She was able to feel her feelings, and later explored her feelings, to see what the root cause is. There are different levels to awareness, and the first level is knowing what you experience in the here-and-now. When you feel the physical sensations of fear, for example, i.e. the tightening of the chest or pounding of the heart, you cognitively label it as fear. This is the first step, and you'll be surprised to notice that it can be very difficult for some people. People have to learn how to identify and label emotions. Oftentimes, children will have trouble labeling their emotions, and will say that they feel "mixed up" or not have words at all to describe how they are feeling. Adults have this problem as well; someone might think of their agitated state as anger, when in fact what they are feeling is fear and panic. Once a person can use this first level of awareness to notice and label emotional experiences, they can find deeper meanings and the underlying causes to the emotional experiences. Maybe it wasn't anger that you felt when that person cut you off, maybe it was an intense sense of fear, because you had an experience in a car accident that you aren't thinking of right now. Sometimes when you are yelling at that customer service representative on the phone, you aren't really yelling at them. You're yelling at your mother, your childhood teacher, your uncle.

At a higher level of awareness, we are sorting these things out- why did I feel that anger yesterday? Was I able to express it appropriately? How was I presenting my anger? Did I keep it inside? Often times there are deep, unresolved issues that we find when we really pay attention to the emotions and thoughts that are happening throughout our experience.

In Katherine and Sam's case, Katherine used her sharp skills of self-awareness to reassess her situation. She knows that she dislikes when people are late, and realizes that there might be another side to the story. When Sam consistently was missing meetings, another, less-self-aware version of Katherine might've kept that feeling built up until they felt like they had no choice but to fire Sam. Katherine stays cool however, notices her anger and frustration, and decides to do something about it. What is it she decides to do? Have a responsible, two-sided conversation about how she is and how Sam is. Sam has at least enough awareness to know that he wants to stay busy but also wants his position working with Katherine. However, if Katherine wasn't able to take the initiative to ask him to explore himself, he may have never gotten there. Once Katherine and Sam are able to establish and identify their personalities, they see the side of the story that they couldn't see before: that each of them have drives, some conflicting and some congruent, and they both have needs, again, some conflicting and some congruent, and that all of these drives and needs are valid. They just needed to identify the problem and communicate with each other about it.

Lets discuss some of the pitfalls that people run into when they're trying to communicate with people. The first is lack of clarity. When you talk to someone about interpersonal issues, or really, anything, it is important to say what you mean and mean what you say. If you would like to tell May that her music is distracting to you, try not to say, "May, that music sucks". You might think that you are making it clear that you want the music to be turned down a little bit, but you're not. Really, you're just mocking her taste, when she may not even know what her actions are affecting you. Obviously, it can sometimes be difficult to make yourself clear, especially if the subject matter is difficult to talk about. On the other hand, sometimes you may need to amplify your concerns. If a Type Two, the Giver, is presented with a problem of a person obstructing their needs or desires, they can sometimes tone down their needs or ignore them altogether. Rather than "hey, do you think you could think about not doing that?" try, "that's not working for me", or "I need to find a solution for this problem." Clarifying your language can do wonders for communication.

Another important aspect of communication is kindness. This can be harder for some types than it is for others. The Perfectionist is a classic example; they can sometimes have trouble keeping their criticisms of others constructive, and can sometimes have a binary view of what is good. They tend to use this judgment on themselves and it leaks out into their judgments of other people. There is a loving kindness that is the tendency of all personality types and it serves as a basic human tendency towards love.

Now, you may find that you aren't always in the type of situation that will allow for a sit-down conversation with somebody about each of your personality types. Of course, every tense interaction we have in a month cannot possibly lead to a meeting similar to Katherine and Sam's, because that is obviously impractical. However, by taking some time to consider why you are the way you are (a quite cogent way of describing what the Enneagram can do for you), you will be able to at least grow an understanding of yourself. From there, the world tends to open up to people. You can use your understanding of yourself to find the capacity to understand others.

For example, lets say you run into a book about the Enneagram of personality. You read it, start to get interested, and immediately recognize yourself in Type Six, the Loyalist. You read a little more, and start to see yourself in a different light. You start to read about the other types, and you have more analytic thoughts. Some of the characteristics in the other types match you as well, and you find yourself labeling your family members and coworkers. This helps to spark a new pattern of awareness around different types of people. You might find that the vigilance you keep is something that you now understand in a different light. This new awareness can serve as a framework for thinking about other people. When there is a difficult or tense situation, you can have a little bit of perspective on what makes you the way you are, and how this person might be experiencing you.

Another thing to consider when using the Enneagram to improve communication is to analyze the communication styles of the different types. Each type has strengths and weaknesses in their communication style. Type One, The Perfectionist, tends to be honest and polite. They might run into trouble, however, when they drift toward their natural tendency to use words that evoke judgment in their communication. A Perfectionist should strive to remember that others don't necessarily ascribe to their standards and expectations, and try not to say that people ought to or should do things. They can be very opinionated. One tip for the Perfectionist to try is to tune into your body language, and pay attention to what the body is saying.

Type Two, The Giver, will be able to listen very well. They are generally good at asking questions, as they enjoy eliciting the feelings and thoughts of others. Type Twos find themselves at home in many relationships and communicate well with certain types. The Giver should watch out to not give out too much unsolicited advice, which they can sometimes get preoccupied with. The Giver often needs to work on expressing their own feelings, whatever that looks like for individuals. By being more honest and in the moment with their communication, The Giver can maintain clearer boundaries.

Type Three, The Performer, is often very confident, and this helps their communication. They are good at communicating about problems and good at finding solutions. It will often be an enjoyable experience to talk to a Type Three. They can become impatient, sometimes, with overly long conversations or emotional conversations. The Type Three Performer often needs to learn to listen to others more. This can be achieved by learning about active listening- asking questions, making eye contact, and showing an interest in a person's talk.

Type Four, The Romantic, can hold conversations that are very deep and intense. They may mirror the Giver in this regard. A Romantic's communication is often non-judgmental and non-superficial, making them adept at finding a person's meaning. Sometimes they can be too intense, however, searching for some deeper meaning where there isn't any. One tip for a Four in his or her communication is to remember that you can't have an incredibly deep connection with everyone; it's just not possible.

Type Five, the Investigator, is good at being respectful in their speech. They usually can find something to amuse them and they like to observe others in their speech and communication patterns. The Five, like the Two, is often lacking in their ability to share of themselves with their own feelings, so a tip for Fives in their communication is to share more personal information and feelings with others and to try not to worry about what others will do with that information.

Type Sixes, The Loyalists, like to have complex conversations. They will enjoy a serious topic, and they'll be able to have a sense of humor about serious things. They tend to be witty and ironic in their speech. They might become overly reactive in some situations, and should strive to be less reactive and more responsive. A Type Six should look to become less questioning of other's motives and to trust their own insight.

Type Seven, or the Enthusiast, likes to tell long stories. When you are trying to follow the logic of a Seven, try to remain open and focused, as it can be easy to lose them. They are light-hearted and talk quickly. They are good at engaging people and keeping them interested in their stories and jokes. A Type Seven might find that they need to tell a few less stories, and ask others more questions to improve their communication.

Type Eight, or the Protector, is often very direct and candid. They can use their bluntness for better or for worse outcomes. They like action and are interested in confronting others and being confronted. The Eight can be a little demanding in their speech, which is something to look out for. They can also be dismissive and become angry more easily than some other types. A Protector should try to listen to those who they don't hold in a high regard. They might find that they have misjudged the person.

The Type Nine, or the Peacemaker, is generally relaxing to interact with. They are generally good communicators, and like to affirm others. They establish rapport easily and make friends well. Sometimes, the Nine will have a low expression of themselves, or they might be ambiguous and indecisive. A tip for Nines to improve their communication is to be honest and open and share their thoughts more quickly with others.

There has been another system developed to describe communication types which can be very usefully applied to the Enneagram system. Virginia Satir was an American therapist and author, who specialized in the areas of family therapy and marriage counseling. Satir has a sizable body of work, but some of her most important work was based in the area of healthy communication. Everybody has their own style of communication, and we all have patterns and little tendencies that make up how we talk to and otherwise communicate with others.

This is true for each of the Enneagram types. Satir recognized five categories, or styles, of communication. These can be seen as an extra level to the Enneagram of personality.

The first category is the Blamer. The Blamer always finds fault in someone else's actions rather than their own. They find that they are never to blame, and that, in fact, someone else is the cause of their problems. The outward expression of a Blamer will be tough and stoic, while inside, they are feeling lonely and scared. Some types that may be inclined to communicate in this way are the 3, the 4, and the 8.

The next Satir communication type is The Placater. The Placaters just want to please. They want everyone around them to understand and agree with them. They are non-assertive, never disagreeing, and always seeking approval. They love to avoid conflict and they care a lot about how other people see them. Some types that may be likely to be a Placater are the 9, the 1, and the 2.

The next Satir communication type is the Computer. The Computer always wants to be correct. They fear being seen as dumb or wrong and hate being vulnerable. They will often outwardly seem like they are very cold or unloving. This is not true, however; inside, they are experiencing lots of emotions, and their inner life is just as rich as the rest of us. The computer wants to remain very calculating and rational. They fall into the trap of being too rational, disregarding their important feelings. They often make value judgements about others without having full information. Types that are likely to communicate in this way are the 5, the 6, and the 7.

Next up we have the Distractor. The Distractor is always looking for attention. They like to be at the center, so that they don't have to live out the hum-drum realities of everyday life. They like to use their emotions as a way to gain attention to their emotional problems, while avoiding actual action. They can be very manipulative at times. The Distractor will outwardly seem charismatic and friendly. Some types that are likely to communicate in this way are the 2, the 7, and the 4.

The final, most self-realized form of communication comes from the Leveler. The Leveler is the model of healthy communication. They say what they mean and mean what they say. The Leveler has emotional balance and they know how to deal with their feelings. The Leveler has great self-esteem and they know their weaknesses and strength. Their words, body, and facial expressions all give the same message. All types have the potential to be this type of communicator. Unlike the other Satir forms of communication, this is something that everyone should strive to achieve.

When you are acting like a Leveler, you will be able to solve problems and be responsive rather than reactive to problems. They will have an intention of positivity behind their communication. They will be able to interpret others' communication and be honest with them. They will be able to have positive beliefs about themselves and be honest with others.

Chapter : 6
Triads, Wings, and Subtypes

There is no point where anyone, perhaps save some monks and spiritual ascetics who claim to have reached enlightenment, gets to the end of personal development, where they are done with their journey and gets to say,

"Now I'm perfect". The key to working with ourselves is to establish a dialogue with ourselves and with our development. This doesn't mean casting judgment upon ourselves, but just paying attention to our thoughts, habits, attitudes and needs. Understanding is part of awareness, and the more understanding we have of the journey of our life so far, the more we can understand how to deal with problems and improve ourselves.

Some psychology theory will be presented here to clarify some of the more complex parts of the Enneagram structure. The character issues and themes in the Enneagram present system of development in the inner triangle of the symbol. There have been many theories of development in spiritual and psychological studies, and the Enneagram is congruent with many of them. The inner triangle connects Type Nine, The Peacemaker, Type Three, the Achiever, and Type Six, the Loyalist. Each of the points also categorizes the nearest two types into the same category, creating three groups of three. These are known as triads. They break down into three previously discussed concepts – the body, the head, and the heart. This mirrors the developmental tasks that we must face in our youth according to the psychologist Margaret Mahler. Mahler's system included the phases of differentiation, practicing (or exploring and testing for danger in the world) and rapprochement, or negotiating one's own need for individuality with the need to have relationships.

A person can go through these stages quickly and all at once in childhood, or it may be stretched out long into adulthood. They may also be cyclical stages, gone through time and time again as a person enters new developmental phases of life. You can see that Mahler's developmental issues match up nicely with the Enneagram's inner triangle: The "body" types are most oriented to the merging that people experience. They have difficulty with differentiating themselves. These types of people may find that they take on the feelings or attitudes of other people too much in childhood.

Points Two, Three, and Four are the emotional or heart triad; points Five, Six and Seven are the mental or head triad, points Eight, Nine and One are the instinctual or body-based triad. The emotional triad is called Attacher, the mental triad is called Detachers, and the instinctual triad is called Defenders.

`The Defenders (instinctual or body, anger or differentiation triad) – Types Eight, Nine, and One are Defenders. They are self-protected; they fight against others or at least move against them when necessary, as a way of making sense of an operating in the world. The Defenders will find that major tasks of development in their lives center around differentiation and independence. Each three of these body-based types will express their search for differentiation in different ways. They will experience conflicts and patterns related to self-definition, and this is the struggle that underlies the core developmental journey for each of these types. Now, the search for differentiation, or becoming aware that you have the power to be independent and considering yourself worthy of independence is a part of everyone's journey. For the Defenders, however, this task remains an issue that they will mostly always be dealing with. This distinguishes them from the other types.

Sometimes our path to differentiation will come and go smoothly, and other times it will not. For the Defenders, this will affect the development of their identity and personality. This is a basic human struggle that is mirrored in our births. Before birth, we are one with another person physically; we live in their body and that is natural and good. The defenders may have a hard time getting over the spiritual trauma of having to leave that state, entering the cold and indeterminate world. We can imagine the infant's perspective at this developmental stage. Part of our development as humans is becoming physically able to live. We must separate from the perfectly symbiotic physical fusion of the womb. If you look at the types extending around the circle of the Enneagram, you can see the process of transformation from totally merged, into becoming more independent and self-referencing.

As infants experience the initial phase of life, they all have to deal with this problem. As the baby develops in the very first months, they have a gradually increased awareness of themselves as a separate human being. The mother's reaction to this process is very important. The mother also experiences this separation, and the optimal situation is that the mother processes this experience and is able to support the baby and also support the child's natural move towards differentiation. Everybody is human and makes mistakes, so it is easy to see how mothers may not always provide the perfect balance of affection and support of autonomy.

This is where many of the Defenders, or Body Triad types, may have experienced a problem. There may have been interruptions to this process or they may have experienced it as highly tumultuous. For example, if there was a lack of structure early in life, the Type One, The Perfectionist, may try to compensate for this by establishing extreme measures of organization and standards to the highest level later in life. Type Nine, The Peacemaker, may experience this stage as a block, and never feel like they completely differentiated from their initial environment. The Peacemaker is often someone to which we can all relate; it represents the essential experience of all humans to a certain degree. Type Eights, or the Protector, may indicate a lack of holding in their personality. They became tough to protect themselves because no one else was protecting them.

The Attachers (emotional or heart, sadness, or practicing triad)– Type Twos, Threes, and Fours – are outer-directed, moving toward people, striving to make sense of and operating the connection to people and relationships. One thing that most Attachers have in common is a defining characteristic that comes from childhood fear. This has to do with separation anxiety.

This stage of development is associated with moving away from differentiation and toward the "practicing" phase, which is the process in which a child goes out into the world to test it, and see how dangerous it is. You could think about a toddler, who loves to explore the world. The toddler, no longer limited to the visual perspective of crawling or lying down, has a brand new vision of the unknown world. This is the phase of practicing the physical tasks that are needed for independence, like walking or other daily activities. There is often a delight that the child experiences in the external world. This can come with some narcissistic tendencies, as to be expected in early childhood.

Some Attachers say that they had an early experience that was very startling to them during this phase. It may have caused them to retreat back into themselves, or to a place of safety. Attachers may not experience an ongoing sense of fear, but they have an underlying motivation for their behaviors that stems from a desire to avoid fear. This developmental stage can certainly provide a sense of overwhelming bewilderment at the world. If you can imagine a child's consciousness at this point, you can imagine how wild the world must seem. A significant part of the practicing phase centers on the individual's experience of their parent as an individual person, rather than a part of them.

These issues are deeply held in the consciousness and subconscious of Attachers. The tension here is between the need to adapt and achieve in a new realm of existence and the need to keep an important relationship. The awareness of this tension grows in the toddler. Then, the child wishes that they could share every new experience and skill with the parent. The child will be looking to the mother to have a sense of validation during this phase, so that the child knows that the mother sees them and approves of their newfound autonomy. Attachers, or Heart types, will feel unlovable and "broken", if they are not shown the sufficient amount of emotional support and mirroring during this phase. Type Threes that are in this situation will find the strategy of achieving to be lovable. Type Twos will find that they tend toward the strategy of giving and adapting to others. Type Fours will strive to be unique, creative, and artistic to earn love.

The Detachers (mental, head, fear, or practicing triad) – Type Fives, Sixes, and Sevens – are inner-directed. They move away from people; they detach as a way of making sense of and operating in the world from inside one's head. This stage of development is associated with moving away from the practicing phase and toward the "rapprochement" phase, which is the process a child has accomplished certain measures of independence, such as being able to walk, but their desire for independence becomes affected by their fear of abandonment. The child, at the beginning of their physical independence, always comes back to the mother. They feel exuberant to come back and share with the parent what they have done in the world. At some point, the child will learn of their limitations; they might run into a particularly intimidating experience that limits their ability to go on. They then have a dilemma between their independence and the proximity to the caretaker. The way that this stage is negotiated successfully is when the caretaker is able to provide sufficient "scaffolding" to support their child in their explorations without the child becoming preoccupied with anxiety.Some Detachers note that they had a difficult experience at this age. It may have caused them to retreat back into themselves, or to a place of safety. Detachers have a sense of safety within themselves, rather than wanting to depend on others for their security. The Detacher has a specific tendency to want to use their inner life to maintain a sense of self, rather than externalizing or depending on others.

The tension from this stage of development is focused on abandonment. The child whose parents did mistook their caution in this stage as weak or ineffectual may have instilled deeply troubling fear of abandonment in the child. It grows a discomfort with new relationships, and the Detacher will always be wondering if their friends or romantic interests will leave them out of nowhere. newfound autonomy.

People make their way in the world as Attachers, Detachers, or Defenders. Now that we've looked at some of the developmental aspects of the triads, lets discuss how the traits of each of the triads manifest in adulthood.

Type Eight, the Protector, is in the Defender triad. The Protector lives with an intense sense of power. The Protector's way of living in the world is by confrontation. This comes from early experiences where confrontation was necessary, even forced upon the, and it helps them to make sense of what matters and what they can do. They deal with the lack of control they had as a small child by wanting to exert their control as an adult. The Protector may have a pessimistic view of the world and move through the world in a suspicious way. They use confrontation as a way of connection. That guy giving you a hard time about going the wrong way in the parking garage? That might be his way of talking to a stranger today. This may serve a purpose for him, whereas you are just annoyed. They can feel when someone is not being honest, because they get scared and want to protect themselves. They like to empower people with challenge and support.

Type Nine, The Peacekeeper, is also part of the Defender Triad. The Peacekeeper likes to focus on the harmonious aspects of life. They like to try to create peace all over, from the workplace to the convenience store. They are easy leaders, but they don't enjoy conflict. This is where they differ from the Protector. The Protector likes to confront others for connection. The Peacekeeper likes to mediate others for connection. They are good at being friendly and laid-back not only with friends and family but also in professional relationships. They are relatively non-competitive, and they believe in the concept of a level playing field.

The Peacekeeper has trouble initiating action, however, and if we compare that to Mahler's first stage, we could postulate that they do this because they are afraid of conflict. Conflict, in early life, was something they had to take on unsupported, and The Peacemaker wants to avoid that. They take on others pressing demands and they rarely express anger. Some Peacemakers may need to do some self-work to be able to express their anger.

Type One, The Perfectionist, is the third of the Defender triad. Their inner voices and life are focused on achieving and seeking perfection. They have a deep sense of what's right. They think they how know how to fix most problems. They often feel that they owe it to themselves to be the most competent. Think about the associations we have with the parents of perfectionists. Often, just like their children, they have the desire for everything to be perfect, and will often push their children into achieving roles. The Perfectionist, then, developed their achieving self, and maybe forgot to develop the self that is just okay, and needs affection.

They can be good leaders and inspire others to reach great heights as well, but must watch to make sure they do not continue a cycle of forced-perfectionism, as this can be very damaging.

Another aspect of childhood development that is notable with Perfectionists is their often severe inner critic, which tells them that they have to be perfection, and that doing something for enjoyment isn't productive. They can have a devastating sense of failure when faced with something they are not able to do. This comes from early messaging from the parent. They may be mirroring the parents' behavior, or they could be just reacting to very high expectations from their environment. Time is the enemy of the Perfectionist, because they feel that they will never have enough time to complete all they need to do.

Let's move to the Attacher Triad. The main mode of being is emotional for those in the Attacher Triad. The types included here are Two, The Giver, Three, the Performer, and Four, the Romantic.

Type Two, the Giver, is in the Attacher Triad. They struggle to know their own needs. They have trouble with differentiation. The Giver is very sensitive to what is going on with other people. They are motivated by others' needs. They are often very good at conveying warmth, knowingness, and understanding, because they do have a genuine concern for people. They sometimes get frustrated because they're not able to do as much as they would like. They get into codependent relationships, and can be obsessive.

We can see how Mahler's second stage of differentiation has influenced the Giver's personality. The stage with which the Giver has become preoccupied is the first one, where an infant is just beginning to understand the difference between "me" and "you". The Giver just wants to live in symbiosis forever, with them being able to help people, and to a certain extent, keep them dependent. Perhaps this is a reenactment of the unhealthy relationship from which this attitude derived, in early childhood, putting themselves in the parents' place.

The Giver will develop an environment where they can help people and get into the type of relationships that give them energy. The well-adjusted Giver will find ways to have their own needs taken care of as well.

Type Three, The Performer, loves to perform; it is as simple as that. Simply and bluntly put, they do this for attention. This is not meant as a reduction of the value of the Performer's pursuits; after all, the Performer often achieves incredible heights in many ways throughout their life. They like to think of themselves as role models. They usually have an excess of confidence, efficiency, and skillfulness. They bask in the applause and approval that they get from achieving.

They can sweep up others in their energy. Deep down, the need to achieve is rooted in the need to establish themselves as worthy of differentiation. It is not enough for a

Perfectionist to be different; they must be the best, or they are no better than the worst. They see an illusion of control, and like to have constant activity and keep away downtime. They sometimes find themselves having difficulty enjoying leisure activities or things that are meant to be fun.

The last of the Attacher Triad is the Romantic, or Type Four. The Romantic has a sense of uniqueness, and they are very comfortable in their idiosyncrasies. They think of themselves as different from others, and sometimes this can lead to loneliness and suffering. They feel that they have a gift that is they. They care deeply about people and look for meaning in life.

You can see how the task of differentiation affects each personality type differently; although each of the Attaches is striving to deal with the primal nature of differentiation, they try to get there in different ways. As for the Romantic, it is enough for them to establish that they are different and unique, and unlike anything else in the world. This soothes their tension of having to be differentiated from others, and helps them think of themselves as people who are worthy of meaning.

The Romantic usually embodies emotionality and drama in their life. Their relationships often take on a dramatic tone. They are relational people; they regard themselves as the type of people who ar e good at relationships.

The issues that the Romantic often experiences in childhood can lead to issues with boundaries in adulthood. The Romantic may get caught up in the feelings of others. They may catastrophize and are very inconsistent in relationships. They have a cycle of expectation and romanticization that always gets undercut by reality.

The final Triad that we will discuss is the Detacher Triad. The Detachers include Type Five, The Investigator, Type Six, the Loyalist, and Type Seven, the Enthusiast.

The Investigator, or Type Five, will often find that they move away from people. They want to detach from the world and realize their thoughts and emotion in their inner life. This makes them feel secure. They minimize participation as a way to keeping themselves safe. This is involved with Mahler's second stage of development, the practicing stage. This is when a child is experimenting with how far they can venture out of safety and still come back to it. The Investigator will always be trying to find answers and make connections in their own mind. They look for extreme approaches to problem solving. They like to look at the world as a puzzle. Each piece might be separate, but together it creates and understandable whole.

In early development, the Investigator may have had issues in the practicing stage. They may have experienced themselves as separate from the parent in this stage, and they realized that perception would be what keeps them feeling good. Perception will safeguard from the difficulties in life. This may be a function of feeling distant from the parents as a young age.

The Investigator is objective and often stone-faced in serious conversations. They like to consider all different points of view and label them all valid. They are very cautious with their time and energy, and can be very good at anticipating the demands of a particular job or task.

The next of the Detachers that we will talk about is Type Six, the Loyalist. The Type Six is has some of the most easily drawn lines to childhood experience. The Type Six regards the world as dangerous and unsafe. They will find that their experience often drives often line up with a pursuit of safety from their perceived threats from the world. They are very good at locking in to what is dangerous. They don't like to confront, and they don't like to escape. They are very loyal, and will often be very good friends. They don't care much about being in positions of leadership. They alternate between being rigid and lax.

The task of Mahler's second stage is autonomy. Autonomy is being separate from the other. At this stage they are developing a sense of differentiation, and the Loyalist might find that at this stage, they may have had problems finding the safety outside oft the immediate connection of the mother, and this will affect their ability to find independence and a healthy sense of self as and adult. They experience time as something to obey.

The Enthusiast, or Type Seven, is very optimistic. They love to think about the world and the future, developing exciting plans. They sometimes have to experience the harsh sense of reality, and may escape into their inner world where they are not limited.

They dislike doing the same thing twice. They like newness, and freshness. They derive energy from stimuli from multiple sources and direction.

They like to plan, and think about possibilities. They will stay late up at night thinking about their next month, how they will travel, or make their world more exciting.

The Enthusiast has a great sense of self, and an Enthusiast who has not adjusted well to adult life may find themselves with a sense of entitlement. They may come across as believing they are entitled to the pleasant life of their dreams. This can be shown through a lack of empathy for other people, placing their needs before others.

What is shown in the Enthusiast's maladaptive coping skills is a failure to have a sense of self, or a lacking in self-concept. This comes from the developmental phase of autonomy that has been previously mentioned.

One meta-perspective on the Enneagram and how we fit into the world is an analysis of the type of personality who thrives in our context (for now we'll be talking about North America, particularly the U.S.). In much of the Enneagram literature there is a reference to the United States embodying the personality of the

Enneagram Type Three, The Performer. The Performer has a deep attentional focus on tasks. It's all about productivity. This attentional focus emphasizes getting things done, producing, and winning. The strengths of this group includes efficiency, reliability, self-confidence, focus on takes, leading, and goal orientation. However, there are many weaknesses that come along with this productivity and winningness. Type Threes tend to brush aside feelings, be impatient, manipulate facts, be deceitful, and believe their own lies. They will detach from soft feelings and demand everyone be productive. Sound anything like the culture of the United States?

When we participate in a culture, we perpetuate its collective myth. The ethos of a country can be identified by looking at the attitudes and ideas refinement in its art, mead, traditions, government, and economy. Say what you will about different economic systems, but the version of the one that we are in right now values some attitudes over others.

One way that this is observed is in the expectations of the gender roles. Our culture tends to value two opposing but symbiotic values: will and love. The women grow up expected to be mothers and lovers, and culture will often tell them that these are the values that should inform what they do for work and in their personal life. Love in this binary system represents empathy; it is the value of being able to relate to a person, understand them, and make them feel like you understand them. The tools that one needs in order to have convey this includes being a good listener, being humble, fiving of yourself, and being unegotistical. This is obviously a positive and incredibly valuable trait, but sometimes these traits are developed at the expense of other traits.

The opposing but symbiotic trait of "will" is assertiveness. Men are told that this is what they must develop at all costs. They must be able to defend themselves, to be leaders, to dominate physically. Sometimes they are told they must learn to dominate psychologically. The tools that you need to develop for this include confidence, a sense of self, and strength. You can see how the development of these traits could engender the under-development of other traits more closely related to love.

When you are examining your personality type and the ways your personality gets trapped or is successful, it is important to consider this binary spectrum for yourself as well. You can ask "how much love am I able to show? How much will am I able to enact?"

When examining these, you might compare them to the expectations of your gender and this can help illuminate aspects of your personality that are difficult to see at first. A rebellious young girl may focus more on her assertive side, because she notices that the world wants her to be a certain way, and she loves going against the grain. This could be the manifestation of a variety of types, for example, this could fit in with the Protector, the Performer, or the Individualist. Likewise, a young man might find that he very severely lacks the qualities of assertiveness and dominance, and that he finds the way he moves in the world is closer to a feminine perspective. A Type Four Romantic can often be this case, or a Giver. Understanding the role that expectations from society play in our development is crucial to giving yourself some context. Context helps us to sort all this stuff out.

Conclusion

Thank you for making it through to the end of *The Enneagram: The Sacred Enneagram in the Christian Perspective*, let's hope it was informative and able to provide you with all of the tools you need to achieve your goals whatever they may be.

The next step is to put into action some of the concepts and awareness that you've developed through the process of reading this book.

Finally, if you found this book useful in any way, a review on Amazon is always appreciated!

Made in the USA
San Bernardino, CA
10 August 2019